W9-BOC-679

Eyewitness
ARMS &
ARMOR

Silver-hilted robe sword, c. 1710

Flintlock pocket pistol, c. 1770

Rapier, c. 1625

Silver-hilted hunting sword, c. 1750

Flintlock "Tower" pistol, c. 1800

Pepperbox revolver, c. 1855

Medieval dagger, c. 1400

Gauntlet, c. 1580

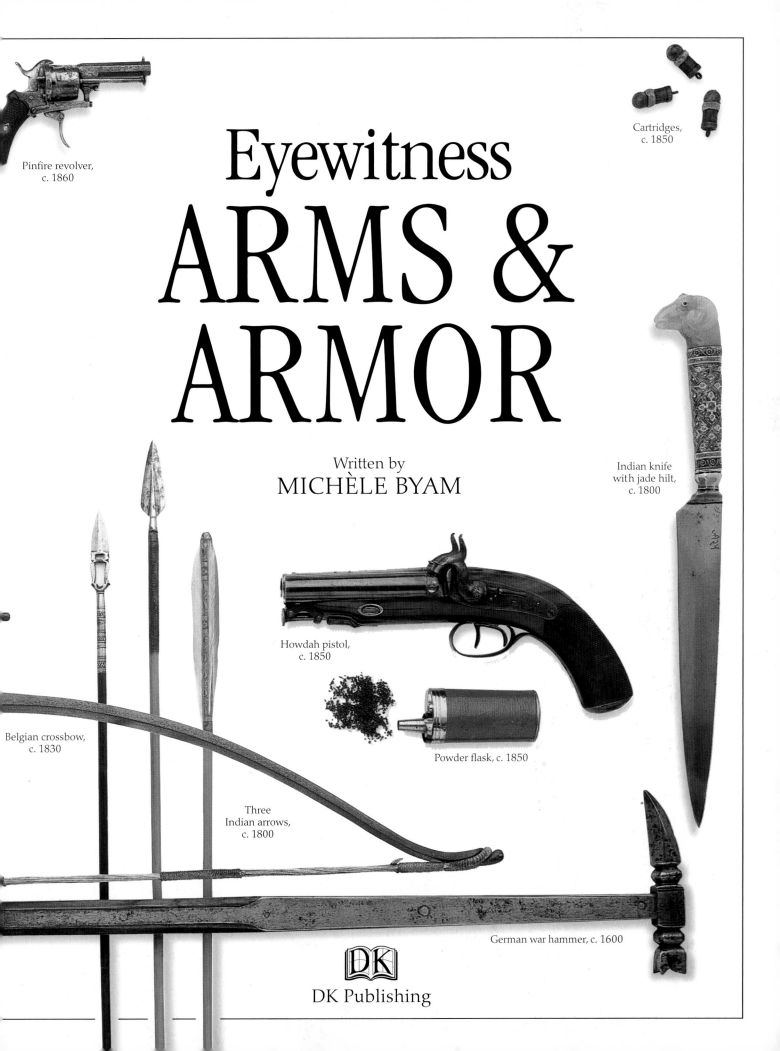

Pinfire revolver,
c. 1860

Cartridges,
c. 1850

Eyewitness
ARMS &
ARMOR

Written by
MICHÈLE BYAM

Indian knife
with jade hilt,
c. 1800

Howdah pistol,
c. 1850

Belgian crossbow,
c. 1830

Powder flask, c. 1850

Three
Indian arrows,
c. 1800

German war hammer, c. 1600

DK
DK Publishing

Maratha "crow-bill" war
pick from northern India

Niam Niam, a ceremonial
knife from Sudan

DK

**LONDON, NEW YORK,
MELBOURNE, MUNICH, and DELHI**

Project editor Michèle Byam
Managing art editor Jane Owen
Special photography Dave King
Editorial consultant David Harding

THIS EDITION
Editors Rob Houston, Steve Setford, Jessamy Wood
Art editors Carol Davis, Peter Radcliffe
Managing editors Julie Ferris, Jane Yorke
Managing art editors Owen Peyton Jones
Associate publisher Andrew Macintyre
Editorial director Nancy Ellwood
Production editor Marc Staples
US editor Margaret Parrish

This Eyewitness ® Guide has been conceived by
Dorling Kindersley Limited and Editions Gallimard

First published in the United States in 1988
This revised edition published in the United States in 2011
by DK Publishing
375 Hudson Street, New York, New York 10014

A catalog record for this book is
available from the Library of Congress.

ISBN 978-0-7566-7319-2 (Hardcover)
ISBN 978-0-7566-8686-4 (Library Binding)

Color reproduction by Colourscan,
Singapore; MDP, UK

Printed and bound by Toppan Printing Co.
(Shenzhen) Ltd, China

Copper dagger of the
Kasai people of
West Africa

Chinese sword in
wooden sheath,
clad in tortoiseshell
with brass mounts

Discover more at
www.dk.com

Contents

Spiked iron
bracelet from
eastern Sudan

Buffalo-horn
knuckle duster from
southern India

Prehistoric weapons

IN ORDER TO HUNT, attack others, or defend themselves, people have always used weapons. In the Early Paleolithic or Old Stone Age, the tiny, scattered communities used weapons mainly for hunting. Early people discovered that if they chipped hard stones such as flint into a pointed shape, the stones could be used for killing and skinning animals. Thousands of years later, in the Upper Paleolithic or Later Stone Age, weapons were revolutionized by the invention of the haft, or handle. Lashing a handle onto an axhead or spearhead made hunting and attacking weapons both stronger and more reliable.

Flint flakes

How hand axes were probably held

BREAKING OFF A FLAKE
The first stage of preparing a flint tool or weapon was to break off a large flint flake with a hammer stone.

STRIKING OFF CHIPS
After the hammer stone had made a rough shape, the remaining core was fashioned into a tool or weapon with a wooden or bone hammer.

PRESSURE FLAKING
A more refined method of working a weapon or tool to a desired shape was by using a bone, stone, or wooden implement to pare the flint's surface.

FLINT NODULE *above*
The first tools and weapons would have come from a nodule, or lump, of flint rock like this. In order to fashion a hand ax, stone flakes were broken off with another stone.

PALEOLITHIC HAND AX,
250,000–70,000 BCE
Although made in the same period of prehistory as the ax shown above right, this weapon or tool shows far less workmanship.

TWO PALEOLITHIC HAND AXES,
c. 300,000–200,000 BCE
These axes or chopping tools, made by an ancestor of modern humans, are hardly recognizable as tools or weapons.

Held at wide en

DEER HUNTING
This old engraving shows a hunter killing a deer with a flint axhead lashed onto a wooden haft

Rough cutting edge

MIDDLE PALEOLITHIC HAND AXES, c. 80,000–40,000 BCE
Both of a similar date, these two hand axes were made by a type of early people known as Neanderthals.

TWO SHAPED PALEOLITHIC HAND AXES, c. 250,000–70,000 BCE *left and below*
Hand axes were certainly used by Paleolithic people as weapons when hunting animals, but we can only guess whether an ax like this was used as a battle-ax in warfare.

Cave painting of bowmen from Cueva Remigia, Spain, painted between 12,000 and 3,000 BCE

Spearhead tip

SPEARHEAD, c. 20,000 BCE
By the time this possible spearhead was made by *Homo sapiens sapiens*, or modern humans, handles had been invented, thus revolutionizing weapons and tools.

STONE AGE MAMMOTH HUNT
Hunters needed bravery and guile to trap and kill large animals. Having been wounded by spears made of sharpend wood and driven into a pit, this woolly mammoth (an extinct type of elephant) is being battered to death with rocks.

STONE AGE HUNTERS *below*
Cave paintings found in European countries such as Spain and France show either hunters or the animals they killed.

7

Missile weapons

ANYONE WHO HAS EVER thrown a stick or a stone, fired a catapult, or shot an arrow from a bow has used a missile weapon. In fact, such weapons have been used for both hunting and fighting since prehistoric times. More unusual missile weapons include the boomerang—the traditional weapon of the Australian Aborigines—and the curiously shaped throwing weapons used by the tribespeople of Central and West Africa. The simplicity of these weapons is deceptive, for when used by skilled throwers they are just as effective as more complex hand weapons.

Stone spearhead

ASSYRIAN HORSEMAN
This copy of an Assyrian carving depicts a horseman carrying a lance, a sword, and a bow with arrows.

Stick is flatter on one side than the other

Flat piece of hardwood

FIGHTING BOOMERANG *left*
The large wooden boomerangs used by Aborigines in war are designed to fly straight. They do not return to their throwers if they miss their targets.

Aboriginal parrying stick

Grip

Aboriginal throwing club

Striking edge

THROWING A BOOMERANG
When used by a skilled thrower, such as this Australian Aborigine, a boomerang can be sent great distances.

PARRYING STICK *above*
Sticks are defensive rather than offensive weapons. This Aboriginal parrying stick deflects missile weapons such as spears and boomerangs.

Club's pointed end

THROWING CLUB *above right*
An Aborigine aiming this wooden throwing club would have aimed to stun his victim with the weapon's pointed end. Some of the wooden war clubs used by Pacific Islanders and African tribesmen can also be used as missile weapons.

ABORIGINES HUNTING
Australian Aborigines are peaceful people who rarely use their weapons for fighting. This 19th-century painting shows a group of Aborigines hunting game with hand clubs, shields, and multitipped fishing spears.

ABORIGINAL SPEAR *above*
Made of stone or bone, the heads of Aboriginal throwing spears are made in much the same way as the spears once used by Stone Age hunters (p. 7).

Protective arrow sheath

Poisoned tip

SHORT BOW
Although bows are popular all over the world, only a few tribespeople make poisoned arrows. This bow and poisoned arrow come from West Africa.

Assyrian archer shooting a short bow

Persian king with bow and arrow

Striking edge

THROWING AXES
Steel throwing axes became popular in Europe in the Middle Ages, but they were used much earlier by certain African tribes. These two axes were made in West Africa in around 1900.

THROWING KNIFE
Among the most unusual-looking weapons are African throwing knives. A multibladed weapon has a better than average chance of injuring its target.

Short handle

THE STAFF SLING *below*
Slings were used for throwing stones by European armies until the 16th century, when they were employed as grenade launchers. The staff sling, a shaft with a leather sling fixed to one end, could hurl stones with tremendous force.

An Anglo-Saxon slinger releasing his staff sling

Holding a sling

The first warriors

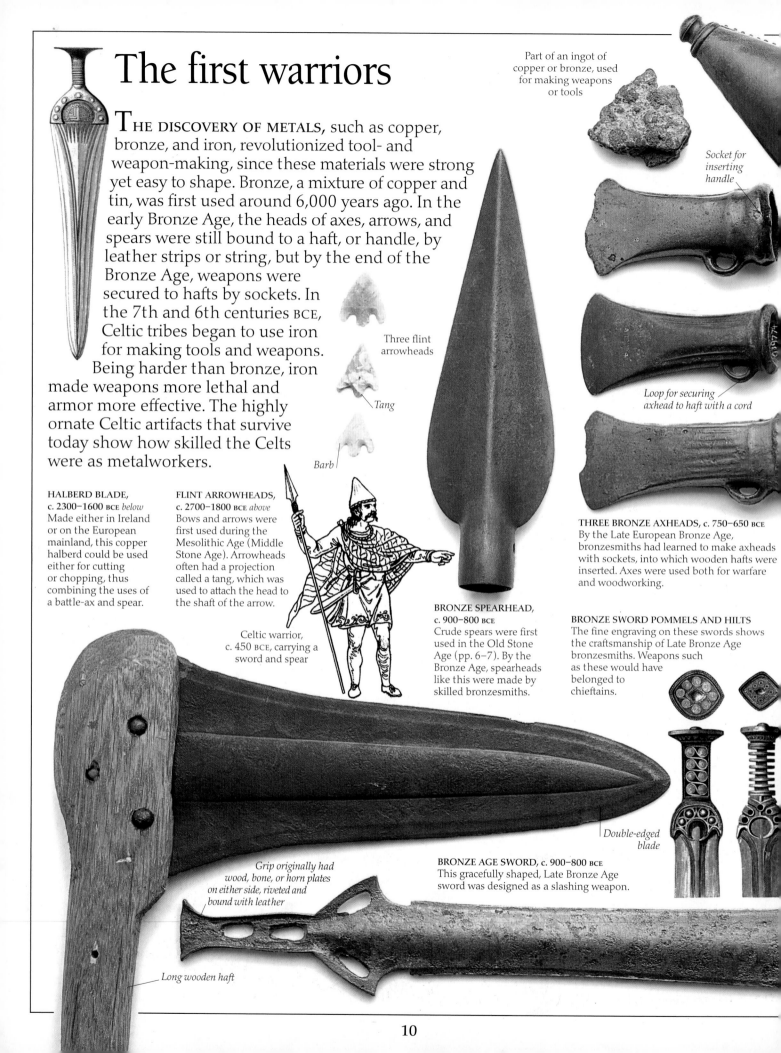

THE DISCOVERY OF METALS, such as copper, bronze, and iron, revolutionized tool- and weapon-making, since these materials were strong yet easy to shape. Bronze, a mixture of copper and tin, was first used around 6,000 years ago. In the early Bronze Age, the heads of axes, arrows, and spears were still bound to a haft, or handle, by leather strips or string, but by the end of the Bronze Age, weapons were secured to hafts by sockets. In the 7th and 6th centuries BCE, Celtic tribes began to use iron for making tools and weapons. Being harder than bronze, iron made weapons more lethal and armor more effective. The highly ornate Celtic artifacts that survive today show how skilled the Celts were as metalworkers.

Part of an ingot of copper or bronze, used for making weapons or tools

Socket for inserting handle

Three flint arrowheads

Tang

Barb

Loop for securing axhead to haft with a cord

HALBERD BLADE,
c. 2300–1600 BCE *below*
Made either in Ireland or on the European mainland, this copper halberd could be used either for cutting or chopping, thus combining the uses of a battle-ax and spear.

FLINT ARROWHEADS,
c. 2700–1800 BCE *above*
Bows and arrows were first used during the Mesolithic Age (Middle Stone Age). Arrowheads often had a projection called a tang, which was used to attach the head to the shaft of the arrow.

Celtic warrior, c. 450 BCE, carrying a sword and spear

THREE BRONZE AXHEADS, c. 750–650 BCE
By the Late European Bronze Age, bronzesmiths had learned to make axheads with sockets, into which wooden hafts were inserted. Axes were used both for warfare and woodworking.

BRONZE SPEARHEAD,
c. 900–800 BCE
Crude spears were first used in the Old Stone Age (pp. 6–7). By the Bronze Age, spearheads like this were made by skilled bronzesmiths.

BRONZE SWORD POMMELS AND HILTS
The fine engraving on these swords shows the craftsmanship of Late Bronze Age bronzesmiths. Weapons such as these would have belonged to chieftains.

Double-edged blade

Grip originally had wood, bone, or horn plates on either side, riveted and bound with leather

BRONZE AGE SWORD, c. 900–800 BCE
This gracefully shaped, Late Bronze Age sword was designed as a slashing weapon.

Long wooden haft

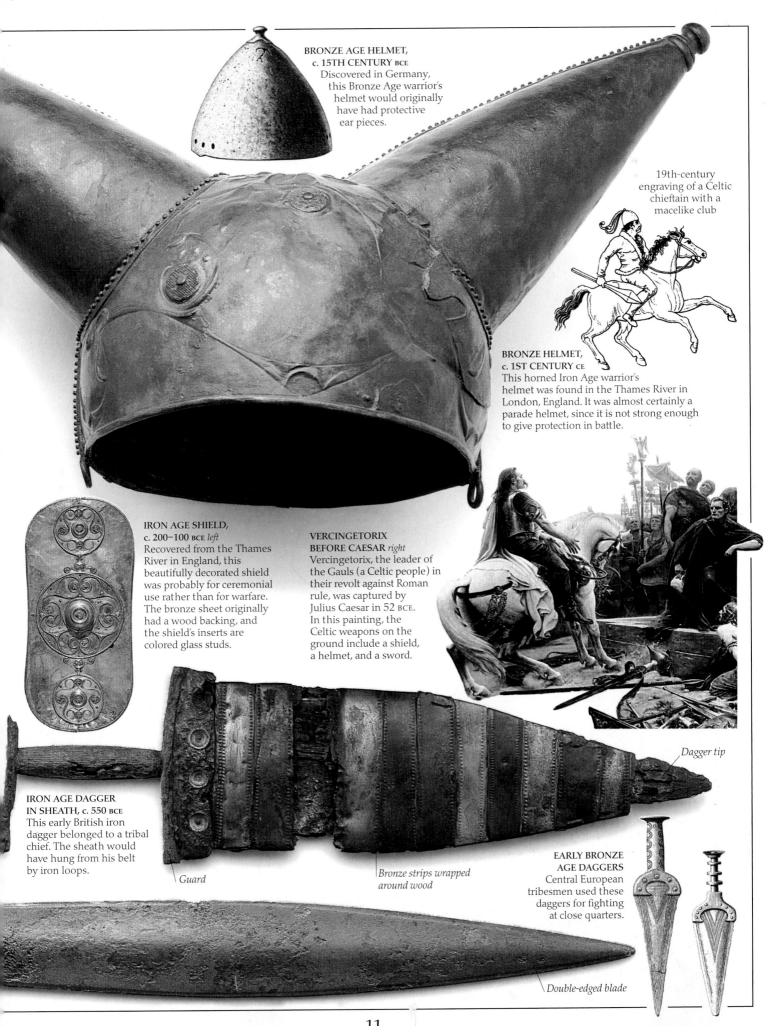

BRONZE AGE HELMET,
c. 15TH CENTURY BCE
Discovered in Germany, this Bronze Age warrior's helmet would originally have had protective ear pieces.

19th-century engraving of a Celtic chieftain with a macelike club

BRONZE HELMET,
c. 1ST CENTURY CE
This horned Iron Age warrior's helmet was found in the Thames River in London, England. It was almost certainly a parade helmet, since it is not strong enough to give protection in battle.

IRON AGE SHIELD,
c. 200−100 BCE *left*
Recovered from the Thames River in England, this beautifully decorated shield was probably for ceremonial use rather than for warfare. The bronze sheet originally had a wood backing, and the shield's inserts are colored glass studs.

VERCINGETORIX
BEFORE CAESAR *right*
Vercingetorix, the leader of the Gauls (a Celtic people) in their revolt against Roman rule, was captured by Julius Caesar in 52 BCE. In this painting, the Celtic weapons on the ground include a shield, a helmet, and a sword.

Dagger tip

IRON AGE DAGGER
IN SHEATH, c. 550 BCE
This early British iron dagger belonged to a tribal chief. The sheath would have hung from his belt by iron loops.

Guard

Bronze strips wrapped around wood

EARLY BRONZE
AGE DAGGERS
Central European tribesmen used these daggers for fighting at close quarters.

Double-edged blade

11

Greeks and Romans

Gladius *hilt, or handle, made of wood or bone*

ROMAN DAGGER
Soldiers carried a short dagger called a *pugio* on their belt at their left hip. Its iron scabbard was often decorated with inlaid enamel patterns. Roman works of art only depict soldiers wearing a *pugio* in the 1st centuries BCE and CE, suggesting that it was not considered an essential weapon.

THE TWO GREATEST ARMIES of ancient times were the Macedonian army under Alexander the Great and the Roman army. From 334 to 326 BCE, Macedonia, a small Greek state, had a superb army built around the phalanx—a dense line of spear-carrying infantry. The basis of the Roman army was the legion—a unit of infantry with supporting cavalry. Between 800 BCE and 200 CE, the Roman army's discipline, efficient organization, and adaptability—constantly changing its tactics and arms in response to the enemy's weapons and the availability of materials—enabled Rome to establish the ancient world's greatest empire. The Roman armor and weapons shown here are accurate replicas of equipment carried by the legionaries, or soldiers, of Rome.

A Roman standard-bearer wearing a *gladius*

Grip made of bronze

INFANTRY SWORD
Roman legionaries were armed with a *gladius*, a short, double-edged sword that was used more for thrusting than for cutting. It was worn at the right hip, either on a belt or a baldric (shoulder belt). The scabbard was sometimes highly decorated, as in this example from the 1st century CE.

Blade with double edge

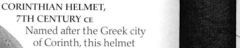

Greek hoplite

The armor of a Greek hoplite, or foot soldier, included a metal helmet, a breastplate made of bronze or layers of linen reinforced by scales or plates, a metal shield, and leg armor.

CORINTHIAN HELMET, 7TH CENTURY CE
Named after the Greek city of Corinth, this helmet style was first made in the 8th century BCE. It gave almost complete protection, since only the eyes and mouth were left uncovered. When not fighting, a soldier often wore his helmet pushed back on his head for comfort, with his face exposed.

Wooden gladius, clad in leather scabbard with bronze decoration

Iron *pugio* scabbard with belt loops

GREEK VASE
Much of our knowledge of ancient Greek arms and armor comes from decorations on contemporary vases. Here, the Greek hero Achilles is shown killing Penthesilea. Painted about 540 BCE, the two figures depicted give a good idea of the helmet styles and body armor of the period.

SCENE FROM THE ILIAD
This depiction of hoplites is from a Victorian edition of the Greek epic poem the *Iliad*. Written in the 8th century BCE and attributed to Homer, the poem tells of the events in the final year of the mythological Trojan War. The warrior on the left is wearing his sword on his right hip, Roman style.

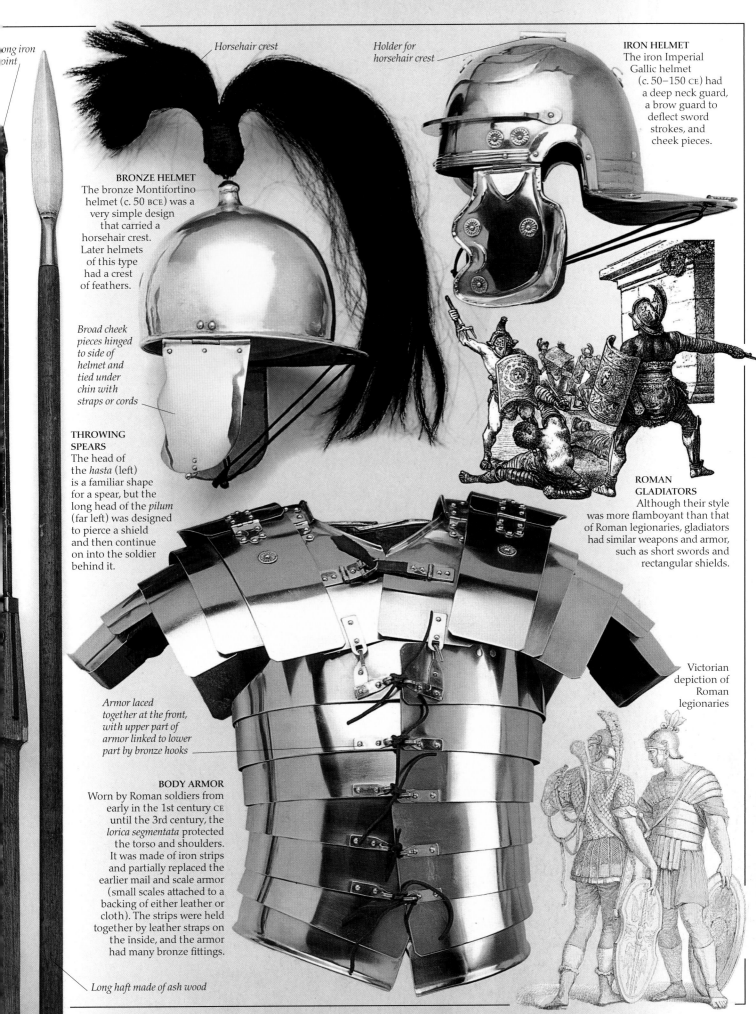

long iron point

BRONZE HELMET
The bronze Montifortino helmet (c. 50 BCE) was a very simple design that carried a horsehair crest. Later helmets of this type had a crest of feathers.

Horsehair crest

Holder for horsehair crest

IRON HELMET
The iron Imperial Gallic helmet (c. 50–150 CE) had a deep neck guard, a brow guard to deflect sword strokes, and cheek pieces.

Broad cheek pieces hinged to side of helmet and tied under chin with straps or cords

THROWING SPEARS
The head of the *hasta* (left) is a familiar shape for a spear, but the long head of the *pilum* (far left) was designed to pierce a shield and then continue on into the soldier behind it.

ROMAN GLADIATORS
Although their style was more flamboyant than that of Roman legionaries, gladiators had similar weapons and armor, such as short swords and rectangular shields.

Armor laced together at the front, with upper part of armor linked to lower part by bronze hooks

BODY ARMOR
Worn by Roman soldiers from early in the 1st century CE until the 3rd century, the *lorica segmentata* protected the torso and shoulders. It was made of iron strips and partially replaced the earlier mail and scale armor (small scales attached to a backing of either leather or cloth). The strips were held together by leather straps on the inside, and the armor had many bronze fittings.

Victorian depiction of Roman legionaries

Long haft made of ash wood

Weapons from Barbarian Europe

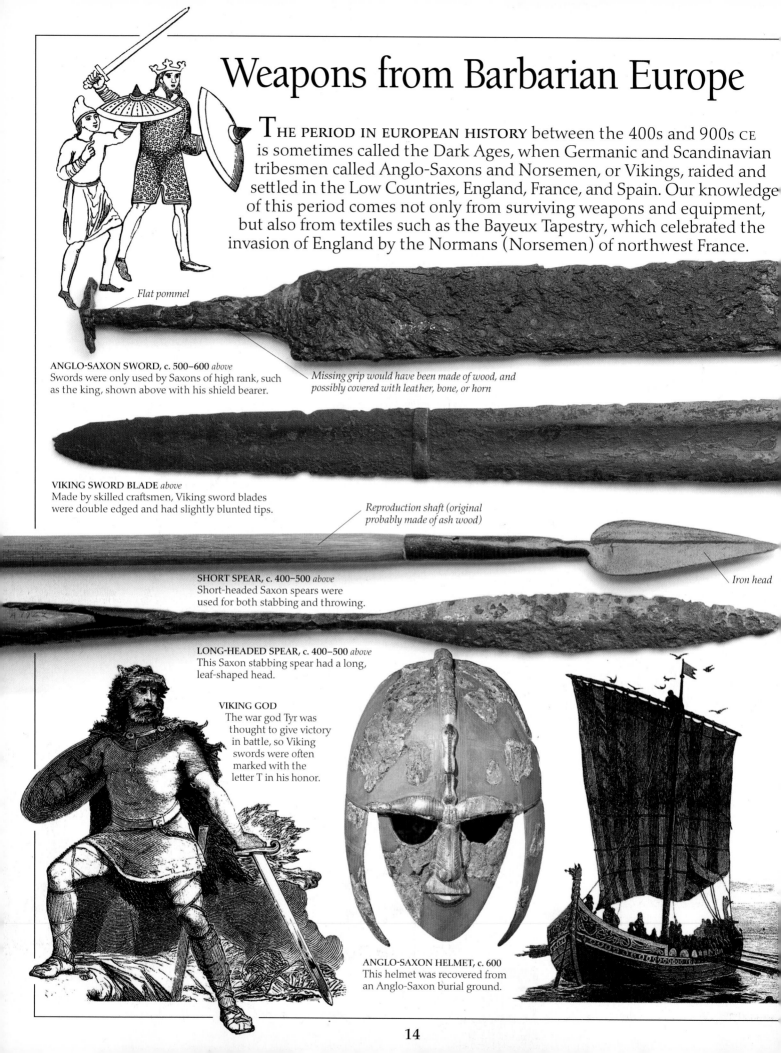

The period in European history between the 400s and 900s CE is sometimes called the Dark Ages, when Germanic and Scandinavian tribesmen called Anglo-Saxons and Norsemen, or Vikings, raided and settled in the Low Countries, England, France, and Spain. Our knowledge of this period comes not only from surviving weapons and equipment, but also from textiles such as the Bayeux Tapestry, which celebrated the invasion of England by the Normans (Norsemen) of northwest France.

Flat pommel

ANGLO-SAXON SWORD, c. 500–600 *above*
Swords were only used by Saxons of high rank, such as the king, shown above with his shield bearer.

Missing grip would have been made of wood, and possibly covered with leather, bone, or horn

VIKING SWORD BLADE *above*
Made by skilled craftsmen, Viking sword blades were double edged and had slightly blunted tips.

Reproduction shaft (original probably made of ash wood)

SHORT SPEAR, c. 400–500 *above*
Short-headed Saxon spears were used for both stabbing and throwing.

Iron head

LONG-HEADED SPEAR, c. 400–500 *above*
This Saxon stabbing spear had a long, leaf-shaped head.

VIKING GOD
The war god Tyr was thought to give victory in battle, so Viking swords were often marked with the letter T in his honor.

ANGLO-SAXON HELMET, c. 600
This helmet was recovered from an Anglo-Saxon burial ground.

14

BAYEUX TAPESTRY

A valuable document on the armor and weapons of the Norman period, the Bayeux Tapestry is a strip of embroidered linen that chronicles the Norman invasion of England in 1066. This section shows Norman horsemen and archers attacking the English forces.

SWORD GUARD, c. 1040

Made of metal, ivory, bone, or horn, sword guards were often inlaid with precious metals.

Inlaid pattern

Rounded point

Shallow fuller (groove) lightens weight of blade

Curved cross-guard

Pyramid-shaped pommel

VIKING SWORD, c. 900–1000 *below*

A Viking's favorite weapon was his sword. Used for slashing rather than thrusting, swords were carried in decorated scabbards.

Grips, made of metal, horn, wood, bone, or leather would have covered the hilt

VIKING AX, c. 900–1000

A Viking warrior swung his battle-ax around his head in an arc before landing a blow on an enemy or his horse.

NORMAN ARCHER

This detail from the Bayeux Tapestry (above) shows an archer with a quiver full of arrows. He is the only archer depicted on the tapestry wearing a chain-mail shirt.

Norman knights using spurs and stirrups

HORSE SPUR, c. 11TH CENTURY

First used in ancient Greece and Rome, spurs helped the Norman knight, a skillful horseman, to control his horse in battle.

Long handle for holding with two hands

Crescent-shaped, broad blade

Cutting edge made of hardened steel

Three Norman arrows (above and below)

Arrowhead made of iron

THE DISCOVERY OF GREENLAND

The Vikings were explorers, as well as warriors and traders. Led by Eric the Red, the Vikings discovered and colonized Greenland in about 985.

Sharply pointed Norman lance

European swords

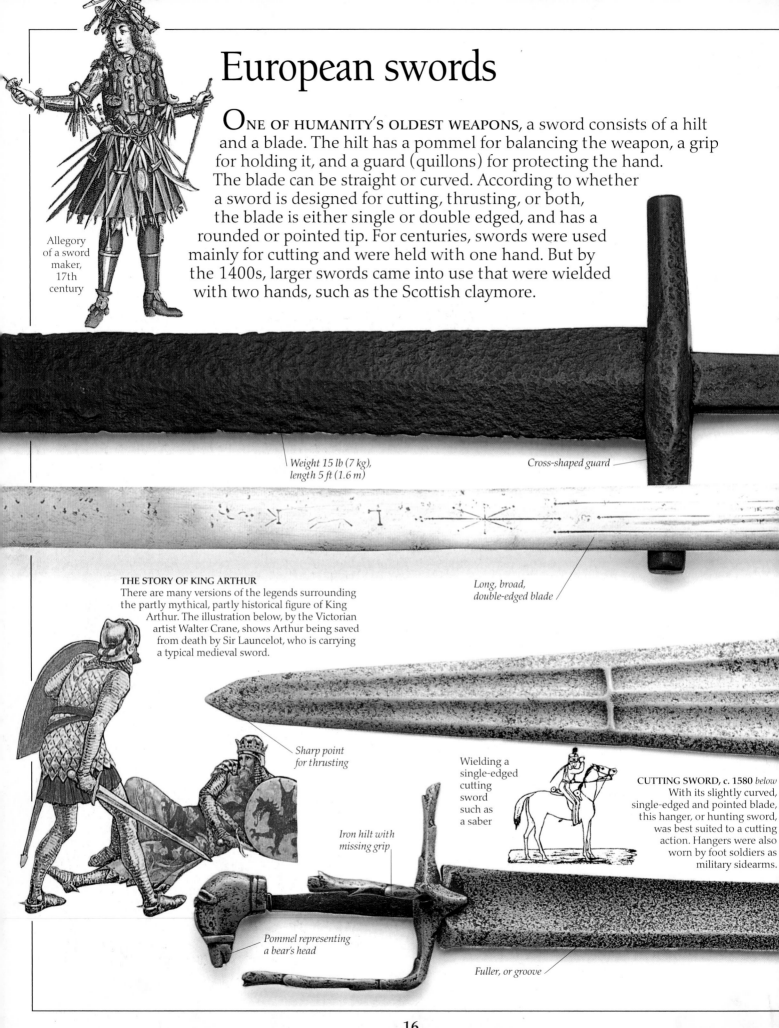

ONE OF HUMANITY'S OLDEST WEAPONS, a sword consists of a hilt and a blade. The hilt has a pommel for balancing the weapon, a grip for holding it, and a guard (quillons) for protecting the hand. The blade can be straight or curved. According to whether a sword is designed for cutting, thrusting, or both, the blade is either single or double edged, and has a rounded or pointed tip. For centuries, swords were used mainly for cutting and were held with one hand. But by the 1400s, larger swords came into use that were wielded with two hands, such as the Scottish claymore.

Allegory of a sword maker, 17th century

Weight 15 lb (7 kg), length 5 ft (1.6 m)

Cross-shaped guard

Long, broad, double-edged blade

THE STORY OF KING ARTHUR
There are many versions of the legends surrounding the partly mythical, partly historical figure of King Arthur. The illustration below, by the Victorian artist Walter Crane, shows Arthur being saved from death by Sir Launcelot, who is carrying a typical medieval sword.

Sharp point for thrusting

Wielding a single-edged cutting sword such as a saber

CUTTING SWORD, c. 1580 *below*
With its slightly curved, single-edged and pointed blade, this hanger, or hunting sword, was best suited to a cutting action. Hangers were also worn by foot soldiers as military sidearms.

Iron hilt with missing grip

Pommel representing a bear's head

Fuller, or groove

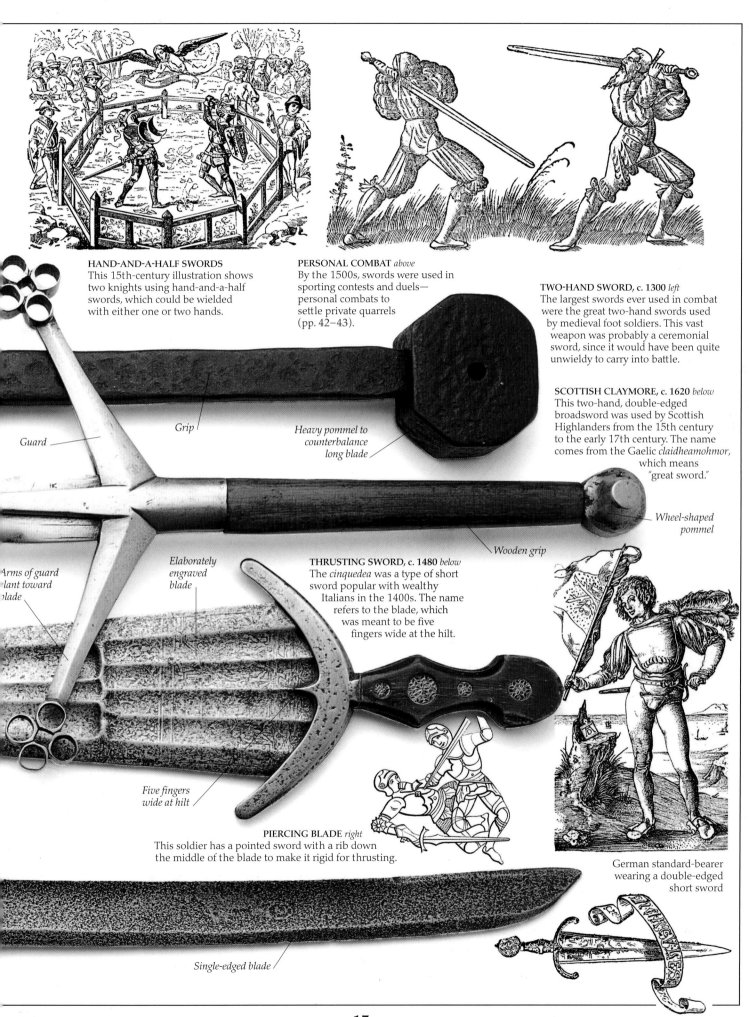

HAND-AND-A-HALF SWORDS
This 15th-century illustration shows two knights using hand-and-a-half swords, which could be wielded with either one or two hands.

PERSONAL COMBAT *above*
By the 1500s, swords were used in sporting contests and duels—personal combats to settle private quarrels (pp. 42–43).

TWO-HAND SWORD, c. 1300 *left*
The largest swords ever used in combat were the great two-hand swords used by medieval foot soldiers. This vast weapon was probably a ceremonial sword, since it would have been quite unwieldy to carry into battle.

Guard

Grip

Heavy pommel to counterbalance long blade

SCOTTISH CLAYMORE, c. 1620 *below*
This two-hand, double-edged broadsword was used by Scottish Highlanders from the 15th century to the early 17th century. The name comes from the Gaelic *claidheamohmor*, which means "great sword."

Wheel-shaped pommel

Wooden grip

Arms of guard slant toward blade

Elaborately engraved blade

THRUSTING SWORD, c. 1480 *below*
The *cinquedea* was a type of short sword popular with wealthy Italians in the 1400s. The name refers to the blade, which was meant to be five fingers wide at the hilt.

Five fingers wide at hilt

PIERCING BLADE *right*
This soldier has a pointed sword with a rib down the middle of the blade to make it rigid for thrusting.

Single-edged blade

German standard-bearer wearing a double-edged short sword

Crossbows and longbows

D**URING THE MIDDLE AGES,** the use of the bow in both hunting and battle was revolutionized by the introduction of the longbow and the crossbow. The longbow, a much-improved version of previous bows (p. 9), could kill an unarmored man at a range of 660 ft (200 m) and its steel-tipped arrows could injure soldiers wearing mail up to 300 ft (90 m) away. Crossbows worked by simple machinery. They were more accurate than longbows, and some had a greater range. Some crossbows were so powerful they had to be loaded mechanicallly, using a crank called a windlass to draw back the string. But crossbows took longer to load than longbows and were more costly to make. Neither weapon had a clear advantage over the other, so many medieval armies used both longbowmen and crossbowmen.

Longbowmen, from a
15th-century manuscript

**SOLDIER USING
A WINDLASS**
Crossbows with a windlass had a slow rate of fire, because they had to be wound to pull back the string before they could be shot. They were most useful in sieges, when the rate of fire was less important.

Archers rained down arrows on the attackers from high on the town walls

Crossbowmen would pick off defenders on the ramparts during a siege

ARCHERS DEFENDING A CITY
During the 15th century, many fortified towns trained archers to defend the city to which they belonged.

Shooting a crossbow

Once spanned—wound or pulled back into its loaded position—the bowstring was held in place by a device called a nut. This was a rotating catch set into the stock, or body, of the crossbow. The bolt was laid in a groove along the top of the stock. Pressing the trigger rotated the nut and released the string, propelling the bolt toward its target.

Steel arrowhead is missing from this arrow

English longbow,
c. 19th century

**ENGLISH YEW
LONGBOW**
Usually made from yew wood, the longbow was a formidable weapon when shot by highly trained archers. Longbow lengths varied from country to country, but in England the bow was usually the same length as the span of an archer's outstretched arms, which in a tall man could equal his height.

Bow consists of a single piece of wood

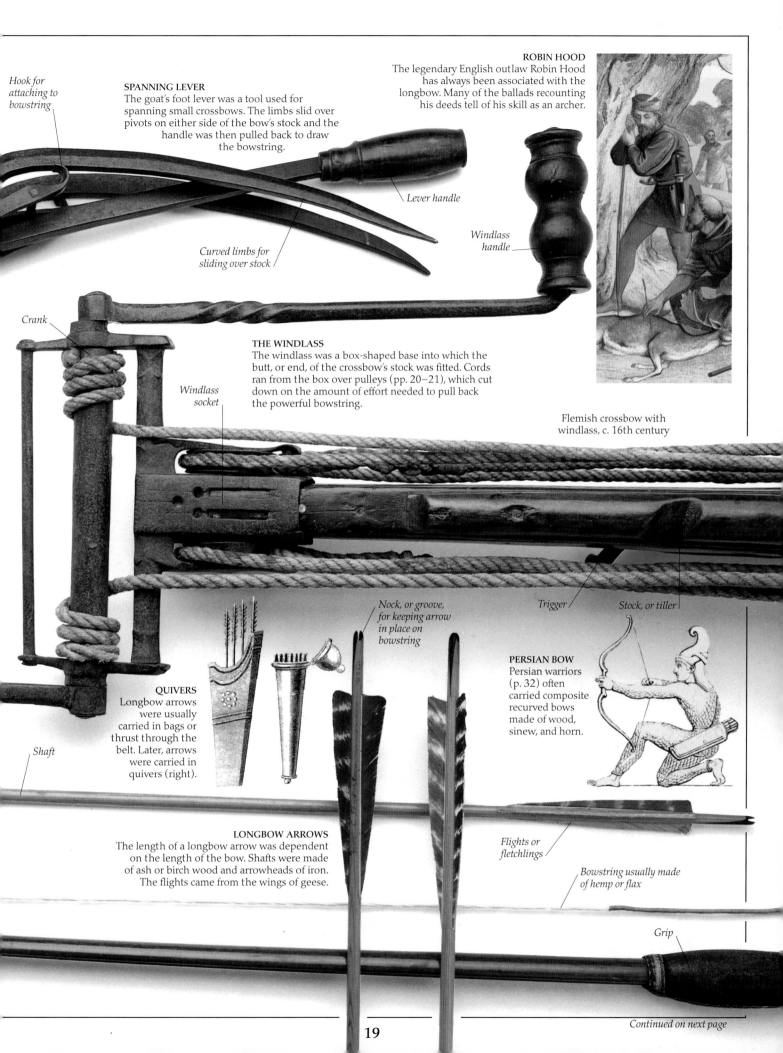

Hook for attaching to bowstring

SPANNING LEVER
The goat's foot lever was a tool used for spanning small crossbows. The limbs slid over pivots on either side of the bow's stock and the handle was then pulled back to draw the bowstring.

Lever handle

Curved limbs for sliding over stock

ROBIN HOOD
The legendary English outlaw Robin Hood has always been associated with the longbow. Many of the ballads recounting his deeds tell of his skill as an archer.

Windlass handle

Crank

THE WINDLASS
The windlass was a box-shaped base into which the butt, or end, of the crossbow's stock was fitted. Cords ran from the box over pulleys (pp. 20–21), which cut down on the amount of effort needed to pull back the powerful bowstring.

Windlass socket

Flemish crossbow with windlass, c. 16th century

Nock, or groove, for keeping arrow in place on bowstring

Trigger   *Stock, or tiller*

QUIVERS
Longbow arrows were usually carried in bags or thrust through the belt. Later, arrows were carried in quivers (right).

PERSIAN BOW
Persian warriors (p. 32) often carried composite recurved bows made of wood, sinew, and horn.

Shaft

LONGBOW ARROWS
The length of a longbow arrow was dependent on the length of the bow. Shafts were made of ash or birch wood and arrowheads of iron. The flights came from the wings of geese.

Flights or fletchlings

Bowstring usually made of hemp or flax

Grip

Continued on next page

15th-century crossbowmen with pavises

Soldier supports pavise while crossbow is reloaded

PROTECTING CROSSBOWMEN *left*
While loading and shooting their weapons, archers and crossbowmen often sheltered behind a large shield called a pavise, sometimes held up by another soldier. By wearing a smaller pavise on his back, a crossbowman could turn away from the enemy and reload in safety. Used in siege warfare between the 14th and 16th centuries, pavises were made of canvas-covered wood.

Mid-15th-century pavise, or shield

16th-century crossbow bolt for warfare and hunting

Wooden shaft

Leather flight

Hemp bowstring

MILITARY CROSSBOW BOLT *above*
The accuracy and deadly penetration of bolts shot from the large military crossbows meant they could easily wound or kill a man at a distance of around 1,000 ft (300 m).

Hook

Pulley

Release nut

Groove where bolt fit

16th-century stone crossbow

English bullet crossbow, early 18th century

Lever knob

LEVER FOR LOADING CROSSBOW
Because bullet-firing crossbows were small and light, their bowstrings could be spanned (pulled back) by hand. The crossbowman placed his weapon against his chest and then operated a built-in bending lever by pressing a knob in the weapon's butt.

Butt

Foresight pillar

Stock, or tiller

Trigger

Bowstring

16th-century, highly ornamented sporting crossbow

BULLET CROSSBOW *above*
Bullet crossbows were popular from the late 18th century to the early 19th century for both target practice and shooting small game. They had double bowstrings with a pouch in the center for the bullet.

A group of 15th-century French crossbowmen shooting from behind pavises

Iron bolt heads

Two 16th-century military bolts

Armor-piercing tip

Stirrup (foot strap)

Backsight

BACKSIGHT
Backsights, situated in the middle of bullet and stone crossbows, had a number of apertures for sighting to different distances. The backsight in this weapon is lying flat and would have been pulled into an upright position for firing.

WILLIAM TELL
Legend says that William Tell, Switzerland's national hero, was forced to shoot an apple from the head of his own son with a crossbow. Tell was being punished for refusing to swear allegiance to the Austrians, who ruled his country in the 1300s.

INCENDIARY ARROWS
Incendiary arrows and bolts were used in warfare until the 1600s. A wad of hemp or flax was soaked in a flammable substance, fixed beneath the arrowhead, and then lit just before the arrow was shot.

Sighting bead

Double bowstring with leather pouch

SIGHTING BEAD
A moveable sighting bead hung between the foresight pillars of bullet-firing crossbows.

Horn nock, or groove, for attaching bowstring

Axes, daggers, and knives

AXES, DAGGERS, AND KNIVES have been used as weapons since prehistoric times (pp. 6–7). At first, axheads were made of stone or bronze, but by the Middle Ages they were usually made of steel or iron, and often had additional spikes or projections to make them appear even more formidable. Most daggers have two sharp edges running into a point and are typically used for stabbing or cutting. Knives usually have a single-edged blade. By looking at a selection of axes, daggers, and knives from all over the world, it is possible to see how different countries produce blades and shafts to suit their own requirements and cultures.

19th-century American infantryman carrying a bowie knife

RING KNIFE
Worn as a ring around the user's forefinger, this curved knife can be found amoung the Bantu-speaking peoples of the Lake Turkana region in Tanzania, East Africa.

Ring placed around forefinger

Iron blade

THROWING KNIFE
This African throwing knife (p. 9) comes from the Democratic Republic of Congo. When thrown, the knife turns around its center of gravity so that it will inflict a wound on an opponent whatever its point of impact.

Wooden hilt bound in leather and copper

STABBING AX
In this unusual ax made by the Matabele people of Zimbabwe, southern Africa, the top of the haft is angled in line with the pointed end of the blade, so the ax can be used with a stabbing as well as a chopping action.

Worn in palm of hand

STABBING KNIFE
This unusual type of knife was worn in the palm of the hand and then thrust forward by the user. It was made by tribespeople in Nigeria, West Africa.

AZTEC DAGGER
The Aztecs, who once dominated Mexico in Central America, made this flint dagger with a mosaic handle.

NAGA WAR AX
The *dao* is an all-purpose ax used by the former head-hunting peoples from the Naga Hills of Assam, India, in their intertribal warfare.

Long bamboo haft partly bound with rings of braided cane

FOLDING KNIFE
In this late 19th-century Spanish knife, the blade folds back to sit partly within the hilt. The blade was locked into place by a steel spring in the hilt.

Hilt of horn and brass

EXECUTIONER'S AX
Executions were usually carried out by one-hand, T-shaped axes or, later, by large two-hand axes (left). Such axes were made only in central and northern Europe.

Plume of dyed animal hair

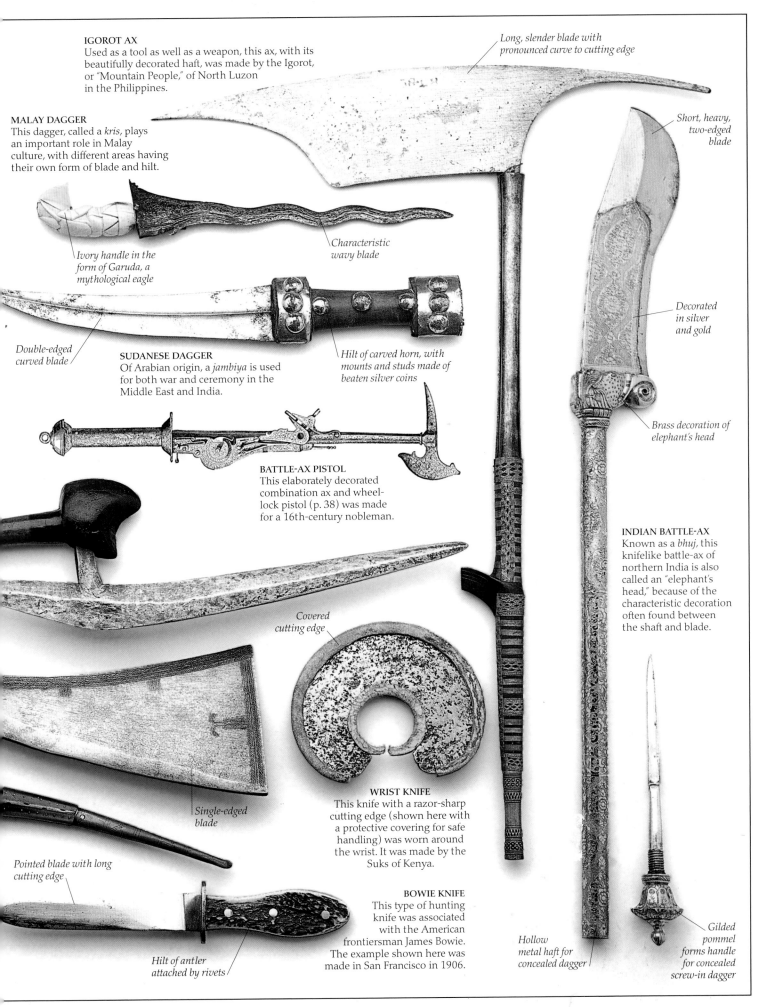

IGOROT AX
Used as a tool as well as a weapon, this ax, with its beautifully decorated haft, was made by the Igorot, or "Mountain People," of North Luzon in the Philippines.

Long, slender blade with pronounced curve to cutting edge

Short, heavy, two-edged blade

MALAY DAGGER
This dagger, called a *kris*, plays an important role in Malay culture, with different areas having their own form of blade and hilt.

Ivory handle in the form of Garuda, a mythological eagle

Characteristic wavy blade

Double-edged curved blade

SUDANESE DAGGER
Of Arabian origin, a *jambiya* is used for both war and ceremony in the Middle East and India.

Hilt of carved horn, with mounts and studs made of beaten silver coins

Decorated in silver and gold

BATTLE-AX PISTOL
This elaborately decorated combination ax and wheel-lock pistol (p. 38) was made for a 16th-century nobleman.

Brass decoration of elephant's head

INDIAN BATTLE-AX
Known as a *bhuj*, this knifelike battle-ax of northern India is also called an "elephant's head," because of the characteristic decoration often found between the shaft and blade.

Covered cutting edge

Single-edged blade

WRIST KNIFE
This knife with a razor-sharp cutting edge (shown here with a protective covering for safe handling) was worn around the wrist. It was made by the Suks of Kenya.

Pointed blade with long cutting edge

BOWIE KNIFE
This type of hunting knife was associated with the American frontiersman James Bowie. The example shown here was made in San Francisco in 1906.

Hilt of antler attached by rivets

Hollow metal haft for concealed dagger

Gilded pommel forms handle for concealed screw-in dagger

Mail and plate armor

Armored knight in a
devotional pose, c. 1250

MAIL—ARMOR MADE FROM linked iron rings—
was probably introduced by the Celts (pp. 10–11)
and became common in western Europe until the
15th century. Mail was flexible, so the links did not
tear easily. However, a blow could still break bones.
Mail also gave poor protection against the increasing
use of armor-piercing arrows and sharp weapon
points. At first, plate armor (introduced gradually
in the 13th century) was simply added to mail armor.
Later, whole suits of plate armor were developed.

EARLY LEG DEFENSE
This Italian relief, from
around 1289, shows
leather leg protection.

MAIL SHIRT
This Oriental mail shirt comprises
solid rings—made without any joins.
European mail was usually riveted—
each ring end was flattened
and linked by a rivet.

POLEAX, c. 1580 *right*
This armor-piercing French weapon
originally had a longer shaft for use
by knights fighting on foot.

Knight wearing mail neck
defense, window detail,
Palace of Westminster,
London, England

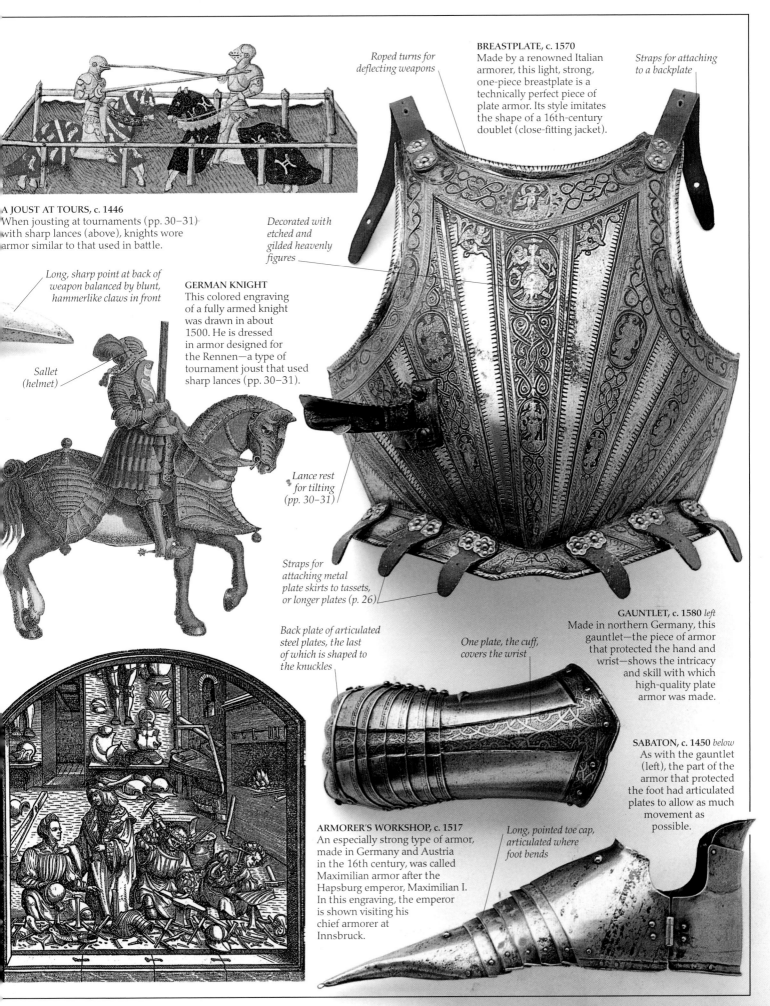

A JOUST AT TOURS, c. 1446
When jousting at tournaments (pp. 30–31)
with sharp lances (above), knights wore
armor similar to that used in battle.

BREASTPLATE, c. 1570
Made by a renowned Italian
armorer, this light, strong,
one-piece breastplate is a
technically perfect piece of
plate armor. Its style imitates
the shape of a 16th-century
doublet (close-fitting jacket).

*Roped turns for
deflecting weapons*

*Straps for attaching
to a backplate*

*Long, sharp point at back of
weapon balanced by blunt,
hammerlike claws in front*

*Decorated with
etched and
gilded heavenly
figures*

GERMAN KNIGHT
This colored engraving
of a fully armed knight
was drawn in about
1500. He is dressed
in armor designed for
the Rennen—a type of
tournament joust that used
sharp lances (pp. 30–31).

*Sallet
(helmet)*

*Lance rest
for tilting
(pp. 30–31)*

*Straps for
attaching metal
plate skirts to tassets,
or longer plates (p. 26)*

GAUNTLET, c. 1580 *left*
Made in northern Germany, this
gauntlet—the piece of armor
that protected the hand and
wrist—shows the intricacy
and skill with which
high-quality plate
armor was made.

*Back plate of articulated
steel plates, the last
of which is shaped to
the knuckles*

*One plate, the cuff,
covers the wrist*

SABATON, c. 1450 *below*
As with the gauntlet
(left), the part of the
armor that protected
the foot had articulated
plates to allow as much
movement as
possible.

ARMORER'S WORKSHOP, c. 1517
An especially strong type of armor,
made in Germany and Austria
in the 16th century, was called
Maximilian armor after the
Hapsburg emperor, Maximilian I.
In this engraving, the emperor
is shown visiting his
chief armorer at
Innsbruck.

*Long, pointed toe cap,
articulated where
foot bends*

A suit of armor

B<small>Y</small> THE MIDDLE OF THE 15TH CENTURY, a fully armed knight was virtually encased in plate armor. However, due to the skill of the late medieval armorer, he was not as restricted as he might appear; the armor joints were designed to permit a large amount of movement. The suit of armor on these pages belonged to a mid-16th-century knight and was made in an Italian workshop. The northern Italians and the southern Germans were the most celebrated armorers in Europe.

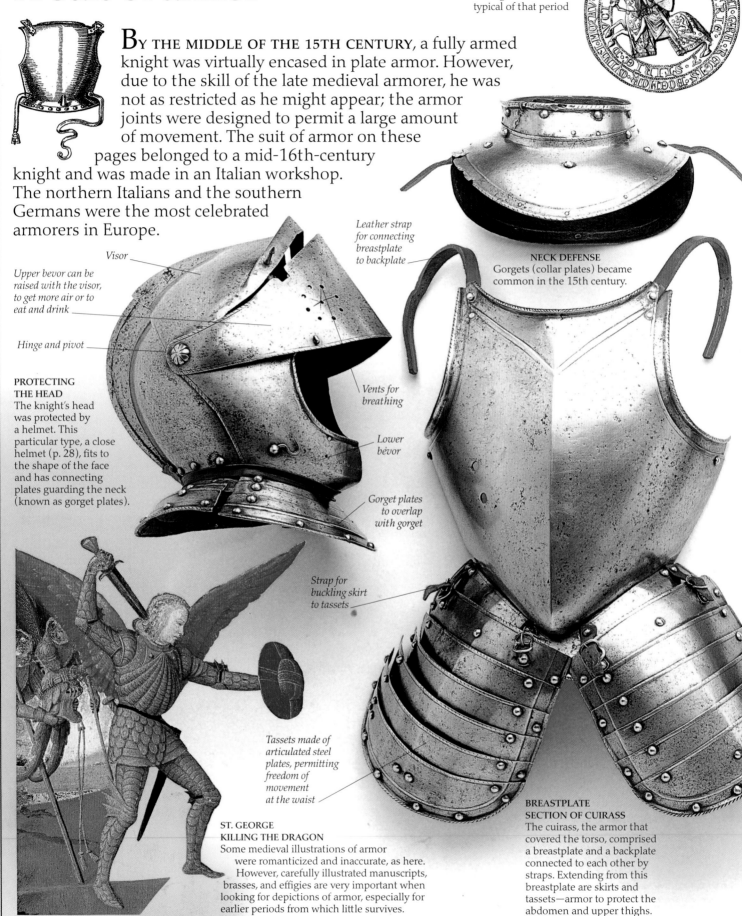

Visor

Upper bevor can be raised with the visor, to get more air or to eat and drink

Hinge and pivot

PROTECTING THE HEAD
The knight's head was protected by a helmet. This particular type, a close helmet (p. 28), fits to the shape of the face and has connecting plates guarding the neck (known as gorget plates).

Leather strap for connecting breastplate to backplate

NECK DEFENSE
Gorgets (collar plates) became common in the 15th century.

Vents for breathing

Lower bevor

Gorget plates to overlap with gorget

Strap for buckling skirt to tassets

Tassets made of articulated steel plates, permitting freedom of movement at the waist

ST. GEORGE KILLING THE DRAGON
Some medieval illustrations of armor were romanticized and inaccurate, as here. However, carefully illustrated manuscripts, brasses, and effigies are very important when looking for depictions of armor, especially for earlier periods from which little survives.

BREASTPLATE SECTION OF CUIRASS
The cuirass, the armor that covered the torso, comprised a breastplate and a backplate connected to each other by straps. Extending from this breastplate are skirts and tassets—armor to protect the abdomen and upper thighs.

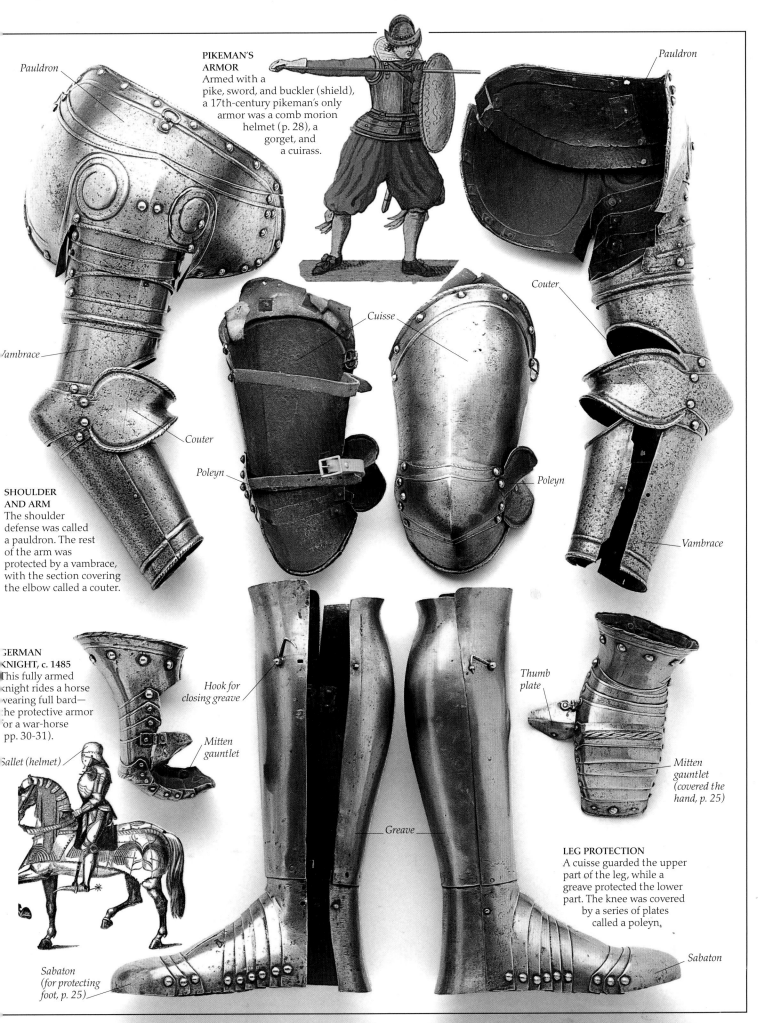

Pauldron

PIKEMAN'S ARMOR
Armed with a pike, sword, and buckler (shield), a 17th-century pikeman's only armor was a comb morion helmet (p. 28), a gorget, and a cuirass.

Pauldron

Cuisse

Couter

Vambrace

Couter

SHOULDER AND ARM
The shoulder defense was called a pauldron. The rest of the arm was protected by a vambrace, with the section covering the elbow called a couter.

Poleyn

Poleyn

Vambrace

GERMAN KNIGHT, c. 1485
This fully armed knight rides a horse wearing full bard—the protective armor for a war-horse (pp. 30-31).

Sallet (helmet)

Hook for closing greave

Mitten gauntlet

Thumb plate

Greave

Mitten gauntlet (covered the hand, p. 25)

LEG PROTECTION
A cuisse guarded the upper part of the leg, while a greave protected the lower part. The knee was covered by a series of plates called a poleyn.

Sabaton (for protecting foot, p. 25)

Sabaton

Helmets

WARRIORS WORE protective helmets as early as the Bronze Age (pp. 10–11). But in the Middle Ages, larger helmets were made to give greater protection to the face and neck. The helm was the first all-enclosing helmet. It was padded inside for comfort, like all helmets, but it was hot to wear. The more open basinet, often with its own visor and mail neck guard, then became popular. A cumbersome version with plate neck defenses appeared around 1400. It was gradually adapted into the side-opening armet. In about 1500, the sallet, another helmet, developed into the front-opening close helmet; soon, the armet and close helmet looked similar. The open, wide-brimmed medieval kettle-hat gave rise to the morion in the 16th century, and then to the pikeman's pot in the 1600s.

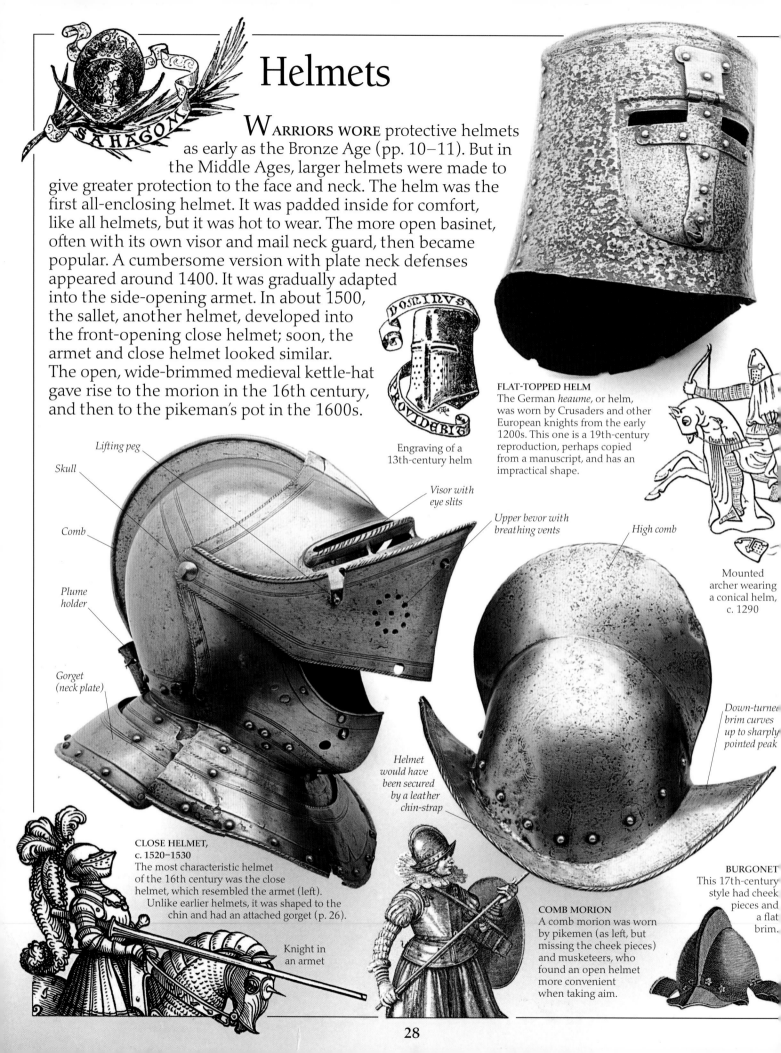

Engraving of a
13th-century helm

FLAT-TOPPED HELM
The German *heaume*, or helm, was worn by Crusaders and other European knights from the early 1200s. This one is a 19th-century reproduction, perhaps copied from a manuscript, and has an impractical shape.

Mounted archer wearing a conical helm, c. 1290

Lifting peg

Skull

Comb

Plume holder

Gorget (neck plate)

Visor with eye slits

Upper bevor with breathing vents

High comb

Down-turned brim curves up to sharply pointed peak

CLOSE HELMET,
c. 1520–1530
The most characteristic helmet of the 16th century was the close helmet, which resembled the armet (left). Unlike earlier helmets, it was shaped to the chin and had an attached gorget (p. 26).

Knight in an armet

Helmet would have been secured by a leather chin-strap

COMB MORION
A comb morion was worn by pikemen (as left, but missing the cheek pieces) and musketeers, who found an open helmet more convenient when taking aim.

BURGONET
This 17th-century style had cheek pieces and a flat brim.

Three pieces of
steel riveted
together

Eye slit

*Breathing
holes*

CONICAL HELM, c. 1370
After the 1350s, the helm was mainly used
for tilting (pp. 30–31). This is a 19th-century
reproduction of a late conical helm. Such a
helm would probably have been worn on top
of a basinet (above right).

*When not
worn, helm
was carried
by this chain*

*Stud for
attaching
visor*

BASINET
From 1350 to
1450, the basinet was
the most common helmet.
Visors (hinged plates for protecting
the face) were introduced around
1300. In this early-15th-century
basinet, plates (now largely missing)
replaced the mail neck guard.

14th-century knights wearing
visored basinets, and a soldier
wearing a kettle-hat helmet

Kettle-hat

*Neck guard riveted to
helmet's skull and
partially shaped
to neck*

*Originally
covered in cloth,
probably velvet*

*Sliding
nasal bar*

17th-century
musketeer
wearing a
civilian hat

*Face guard
formed of three
vertical bars*

*Cheek
piece*

ENGLISH POT, c. 1630–1650
This type of helmet from
the mid-17th century
was devised in Germany,
where it was called a
zischagge (right). It had a laminated
neck guard and a sliding nose guard.
The English version (above and
left)—the English or lobster-tailed
pot—had a face guard, neck guard,
and hinged cheek pieces.

German soldier in
a *zischagge*

IRON HAT, c. 1640–1650
An unusual helmet is this
high-crowned iron hat with a
sliding nasal bar, occasionally
worn by horsemen during the
English Civil War. Originally
covered in material and with
a plume, it would have looked
like a civilian hat of the time.

Tilting armor

THE EARLIEST TOURNAMENTS—mock battles between mounted knights—probably began in the 1100s as a form of rehearsal for war. But by the 1400s, they had evolved into important and colorful social events at which knights displayed their fighting skills and courage before their monarch and their peers. In the 13th century, jousts appeared in which two mounted knights charged at each other with lances. From about 1430, the knights were separated by a barrier called a tilt—hence the word "tilting." Special armor was made for knights taking part in this and other forms of contest to protect the left (or target) side of the body.

French knight tilting with a lance

COATS OF ARMS
Tournament contestants were identified by the insignia on their shields and tunics. Originally shown on the surcoats worn over mail, the insignia became known as "coats of arms."

PARADE HELMET, c. 1630
This bronze helmet with its grotesque human face mask was probably used for the parades that took place in 17th-century tournaments, which had become chiefly displays of horsemanship.

A JOUSTING CONTEST
By the 16th century, tournaments were accompanied by much formal pageantry. The lists, or field, was enclosed by barriers and overlooked by pavilions from which royalty and other notables could watch. This depiction of a tournament shows King Henry VIII tilting with one of his knights, watched by his queen.

TILTING SPUR
Horsemen wear spurs on their heels to urge their horses into action. By the 1500s, tilting spurs often had rowels with strong, sharp spikes, which the knights used to prod their horses into a charge.

Rowel

30

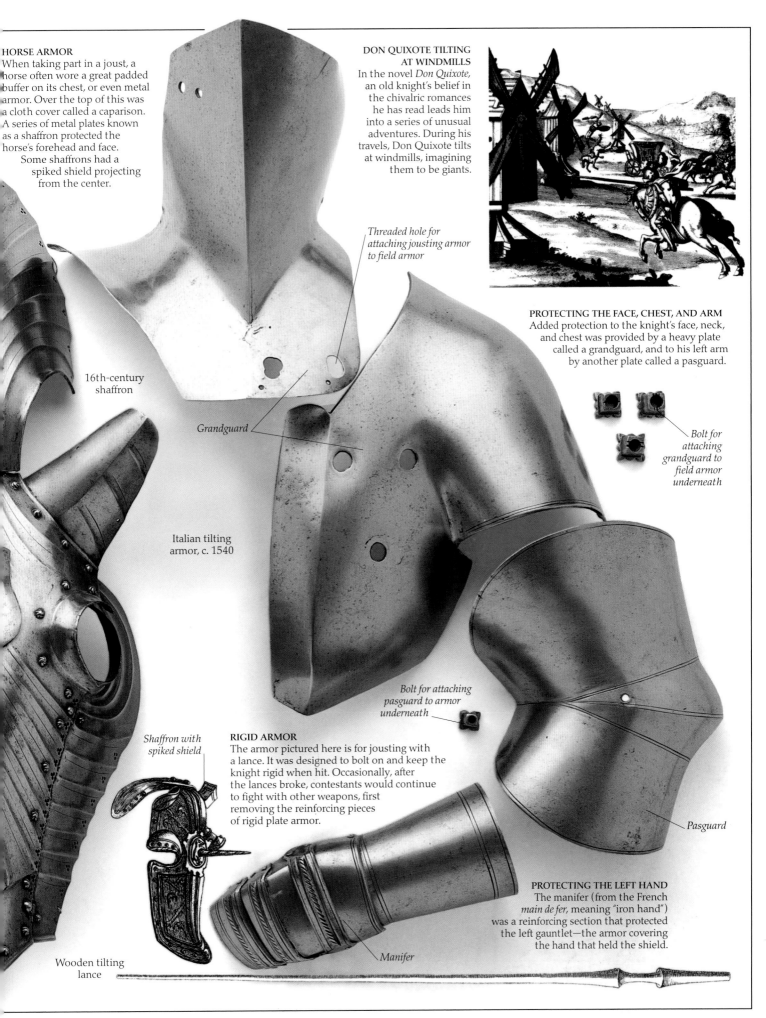

HORSE ARMOR

When taking part in a joust, a horse often wore a great padded buffer on its chest, or even metal armor. Over the top of this was a cloth cover called a caparison. A series of metal plates known as a shaffron protected the horse's forehead and face.

Some shaffrons had a spiked shield projecting from the center.

16th-century shaffron

Threaded hole for attaching jousting armor to field armor

Grandguard

Italian tilting armor, c. 1540

DON QUIXOTE TILTING AT WINDMILLS

In the novel *Don Quixote*, an old knight's belief in the chivalric romances he has read leads him into a series of unusual adventures. During his travels, Don Quixote tilts at windmills, imagining them to be giants.

PROTECTING THE FACE, CHEST, AND ARM

Added protection to the knight's face, neck, and chest was provided by a heavy plate called a grandguard, and to his left arm by another plate called a pasguard.

Bolt for attaching grandguard to field armor underneath

Bolt for attaching pasguard to armor underneath

Shaffron with spiked shield

RIGID ARMOR

The armor pictured here is for jousting with a lance. It was designed to bolt on and keep the knight rigid when hit. Occasionally, after the lances broke, contestants would continue to fight with other weapons, first removing the reinforcing pieces of rigid plate armor.

Pasguard

PROTECTING THE LEFT HAND

The manifer (from the French *main de fer*, meaning "iron hand") was a reinforcing section that protected the left gauntlet—the armor covering the hand that held the shield.

Manifer

Wooden tilting lance

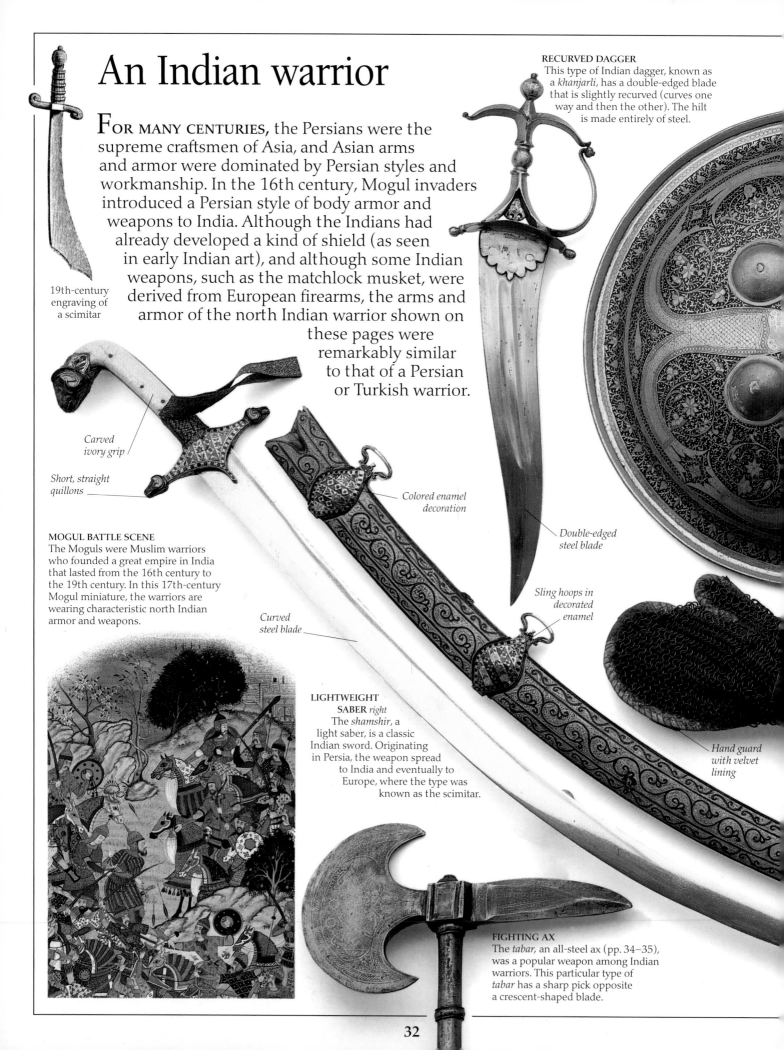

An Indian warrior

FOR MANY CENTURIES, the Persians were the supreme craftsmen of Asia, and Asian arms and armor were dominated by Persian styles and workmanship. In the 16th century, Mogul invaders introduced a Persian style of body armor and weapons to India. Although the Indians had already developed a kind of shield (as seen in early Indian art), and although some Indian weapons, such as the matchlock musket, were derived from European firearms, the arms and armor of the north Indian warrior shown on these pages were remarkably similar to that of a Persian or Turkish warrior.

19th-century engraving of a scimitar

RECURVED DAGGER
This type of Indian dagger, known as a *khanjarli*, has a double-edged blade that is slightly recurved (curves one way and then the other). The hilt is made entirely of steel.

Carved ivory grip

Short, straight quillons

Colored enamel decoration

Double-edged steel blade

MOGUL BATTLE SCENE
The Moguls were Muslim warriors who founded a great empire in India that lasted from the 16th century to the 19th century. In this 17th-century Mogul miniature, the warriors are wearing characteristic north Indian armor and weapons.

Curved steel blade

Sling hoops in decorated enamel

Hand guard with velvet lining

LIGHTWEIGHT SABER *right*
The *shamshir*, a light saber, is a classic Indian sword. Originating in Persia, the weapon spread to India and eventually to Europe, where the type was known as the scimitar.

FIGHTING AX
The *tabar*, an all-steel ax (pp. 34–35), was a popular weapon among Indian warriors. This particular type of *tabar* has a sharp pick opposite a crescent-shaped blade.

CIRCULAR STEEL SHIELD
By the 18th century, Indian and Persian soldiers used a round shield (*dhal* or *sipar*) made of steel or hide (pp. 34–35). Four bosses covered the attachment of the handles for carrying the shield on the left arm.

Boss

Made of steel, with chiseled and gilded decoration

North Indian shield, c. 19th century

NORTH INDIAN HELMET
Known as a *top*, this Indian helmet had mail curtains called aventails that descended to the shoulders. The helmet was secured under the chin with a braided tie.

Spike socket (spike missing)

Socket for feather or tinsel plume (plume missing)

Sliding nasal bar for protecting nose

Aventail to protect the neck, shoulders, and part of the face

INDIAN WARRIORS
These Rajput warriors, photographed in 1857, are armed with a *dhal* (shield), a *tulwar* (sword), and a *bandukh toradar* (matchlock musket).

Mail shoulder straps with metal clasps

ARM GUARD
The tubular vambrace, or *dastana*, was fastened to the arm with straps. The mail extension is to protect the hand.

RECTANGULAR BREASTPLATE
The Indian cuirass, known as a *char aina* (Persian for "four mirrors"), consisted of a light breastplate, a backplate, and two side plates, all of which were shaped to fit on top of the warrior's mail shirt.

Wooden shamshir scabbard bound in tooled leather

Decorated in gold and silver

Lined gold trellis pattern

Indian weapons

(pp. 32–33)

DESPITE THE FOREIGN INFLUENCE on Indian arms and armor (pp. 32–33), some Indian states and peoples developed their own specialized weapons, which they continued to use, alongside Indo-Persian swords and European-style muskets, up until the beginning of the 20th century. These local weapons, which were often beautifully decorated, included the *katar*, the Hindu thrusting dagger, and the *chakram*, the steel war quoit worn by Sikh warriors on their turbans.

Sikh soldier using a flintlock musket, c. 1846

Jade handle inlaid with rubies and diamonds

MULTIARMED GOD *top*
This painting depicts a well-armed Hindu god. His weapons include an ax, a thrusting dagger, tridents, armor-piercing daggers, a mace, and a spear.

ARMOR-PIERCING DAGGER
The *pesh-kabz* was a specialized dagger from Persia and northern India, used mainly for piercing mail. The blade, with a thick, blunt back edge, has a cutting fore edge that tapers to a sharp point.

Dagger screws into hollow ax haft

Hollow handle for dagger

ALL-STEEL BATTLE-AX *above*
This type of *tabar* (p. 32) has an elongated blade with a slightly rounded cutting edge. Its hollow handle conceals a dagger.

Gold decorated steel hilt

SINGLE-EDGED SWORD *below*
The *tulwar* was a curved sword that was widely used in India. This one has the short grip and dishlike pommel characteristic of the Punjab region.

INDIAN WARRIORS IN BATTLE
In this Mogul (p. 32) battle scene every combatant carries a *katar*, or thrusting dagger. There is also the type of Indian sword, the *tulwar*, and some soldiers are carrying the shield known as a *dhal*. Other weapons being used are a bow and arrows, a spear, and a musket.

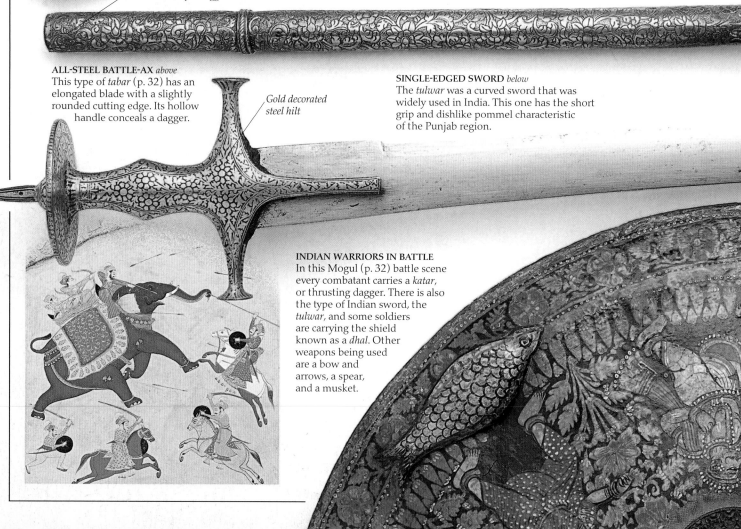

Made of
carved
wood

MATCHLOCK POWDER FLASK
Bandukh toradars, or matchlock muskets
(p. 38), were used in certain parts of
India until the early 20th century. This
painted and gilded matchlock powder
flask, carved in the shape of a fish, has a
Hindu goddess coming out of its mouth.

WAR QUOIT
Used mostly by the Sikhs of
northwest India, the *chakram* is a
flat steel quoit with a razor-sharp
outer edge. Several quoits were worn
around a tall, conical turban and were
either whirled around the forefinger
before throwing or held between the
thumb and forefinger and
thrown underarm.

Hindu
goddess

Sharpened
outer edge

Rounded
inner edge

Rounded
cutting edge

Sikh soldier
spinning a *chakram*
around his forefinger

Inlaid with
silver and gilt

Square
hammerhead

Curved,
single-edged blade

Large,
double-edged
blade

THRUSTING DAGGER
The Hindu dagger, the *katar*, is
found only in India. Made entirely
of steel, it has an H-shaped
handle that is gripped by
the fist. The *katar* is used
at close quarters with
a punching action.

Metal strips
protect
wrist

HIDE SHIELD
This type of *dhal*
(pp. 32–33) is made
of hide and is
decorated with
paintings of
Hindu gods.

Two parallel bars
form grip

A Japanese samurai

A *tsuba* (or sword guard)

JAPANESE WEAPONS and armor are unique. Developed over many centuries, the armor is highly decorative, especially the ornamental type worn by the aristocratic warriors known as samurai (Japanese for "one who serves"). The samurai code of honor dominated Japanese military life from the 12th century until 1868, when the samurai class was abolished. Japanese weapons are well constructed, especially the swords, which are the finest ever made.

Wakizashi scabbard (a *saya*), made of lacquered wood

Wooden sheath for head of spear

Blade made by covering a soft iron core with layers of steel

Metal collar to protect join in a decorative manner

Large crayfish design in black lacquer

Mosaic design made from mother of pearl

Silken cord for securing sword to girdle

Kabuto *helmet with horn-shaped crest*

Flecked, lacquered sheath

Lacquered hilt

Known as tsuba, *Japanese sword guards are collectors' items (see top left)*

Hilt made of wood covered with fish skin and bound with a flat braid

DAGGER
This is an example of the typical Japanese dagger (the *tanto*), with its single-edged blade.

SHORT SWORD
A samurai carried both a short and a long sword. This 17th-century sword is a *wakizashi*, a short sword used not only as an additional fighting sword, but also for the ritual suicide, *seppuku*.

FOOT SOLDIER
This 19th-century foot soldier wears a light cuirass (p. 26), or breastplate, with skirts (*kasazuri*) to protect his lower torso. Earlier cuirasses were not made from a solid sheet, but comprised many small plates laced together.

SCABBARD FITTINGS
A small knife known as the *kozuka* (left) and a skewer, the *kogai* (far left), were carried on either side of the *tanto* (dagger) and sword scabbards.

Hand guard, or half-gauntlet, with leather lining and loops for fingers

SPEAR
Short-bladed spears (*yari*) were carried by horsemen. Foot soldiers carried longer-bladed *yari* (see right).

A SAMURAI COMBAT
This early 19th-century print shows a sword fight between two samurai using long swords called *katana*. Their secondary swords, or *wakizashi*, are tucked through the girdles around their waists.

Opening (tehen) *for warrior's pigtail to pass through*

Helmet bowl (hachi) *made of riveted plates*

Wings, or protective flaps, known as the fukigayeshi

Decorated with brass and lacquer

The maidate—*socket for helmet crest*

Cord for attaching mask to helmet

Hempen moustache

Neck guard (nowdawa) *fastened at the back by cords*

Laminated neck guard (shikoro)

WAR MASK
Warriors wore different types of *mempo*, or war mask, such as this half-mask with a nose piece. Masks not only secured the helmet firmly to the head, but also gave the wearer a more frightening appearance.

Japanese general wearing a *kabuto* helmet bearing a helmet crest, or *kashira-date*

SAMURAI HELMET
Known generally as *kabuto*, Japanese helmets changed continually until the 19th century, with each period having its own distinct features and design. The *kabuto* was secured to the head by cords attached to the brim.

ARMORED SLEEVE
A type of vambrace (p. 27), the armored sleeve (*kote*) protected the arm from spears and swords. Made of close-fitting material, it was laced over the arm and tied around the chest.

Made of silk overlaid with mail connecting metal plates

Early firearms

GUNPOWDER WAS USED IN EUROPE in the 14th century, but it was not until the 16th century that handheld firearms began to fulfil their potential. Giving the firearm a wooden stock, or body, helped the firer to aim, absorb the recoil, and hold the hot barrel, while a lock, or ignition mechanism, let him fire at just the right moment. The simple matchlock plunged a smouldering rope called a slow-match into a small pan of priming powder at the touch of a trigger. A later form of ignition, the wheel-lock, went one stage further, by generating sparks at the moment of firing. Since it was too expensive to replace the matchlock entirely for the common soldier, both systems were used until they were replaced by the more efficient flintlock (pp. 40–41).

HEAVY CAVALRYMAN
Wheel-lock pistols were the first small arms carried by cavalrymen.

Cock, or "dog," holding iron pyrites

Brass butt-cap

Stock inlaid with brass and mother of pearl

Wheel

Stock shaped to fit wheel

LOADING SEQUENCE
Matchlocks may look simple, but they had to be loaded in a strict sequence to prevent misfiring or personal injury. On the left are a few of the loading and firing actions taught to soldiers using these early firearms.

"March, and with your musket carry your rest"

"Poise your musket"

"Shorten your scouring stick"

"Try your match"

"Give fire"

The matchlock

This matchlock is a typical infantry musket of the early 17th century. The pan cover was opened just before taking aim. On pulling the trigger, the lock thrust the tip of the match into the pan to ignite the priming powder, and a flash went through a small touch-hole in the barrel wall to set off the main charge.

OBSCURING THE TARGET
One disadvantage of the original black gunpowder was the dense white smoke it produced, which often obscured the target and prevented a deliberate aim.

Priming pan and cover

Rope slow-match

German matchlock musket, c. early 17th century

Wooden stock

Trigger guard

Trigger

The wheel-lock

This lock produced sparks by holding a piece of iron pyrites against the serrated edge of a spinning wheel, which protruded through the bottom of the priming pan. Just below the pan was a square spindle on which a key was fitted. As the key was turned, a short chain attached to the mainspring caused it to wind up. After the cock, or "dog," was lowered into the pan, the wheel was released. As it spun against the pyrites, it sent a shower of sparks into the pan, setting off the priming and main charge.

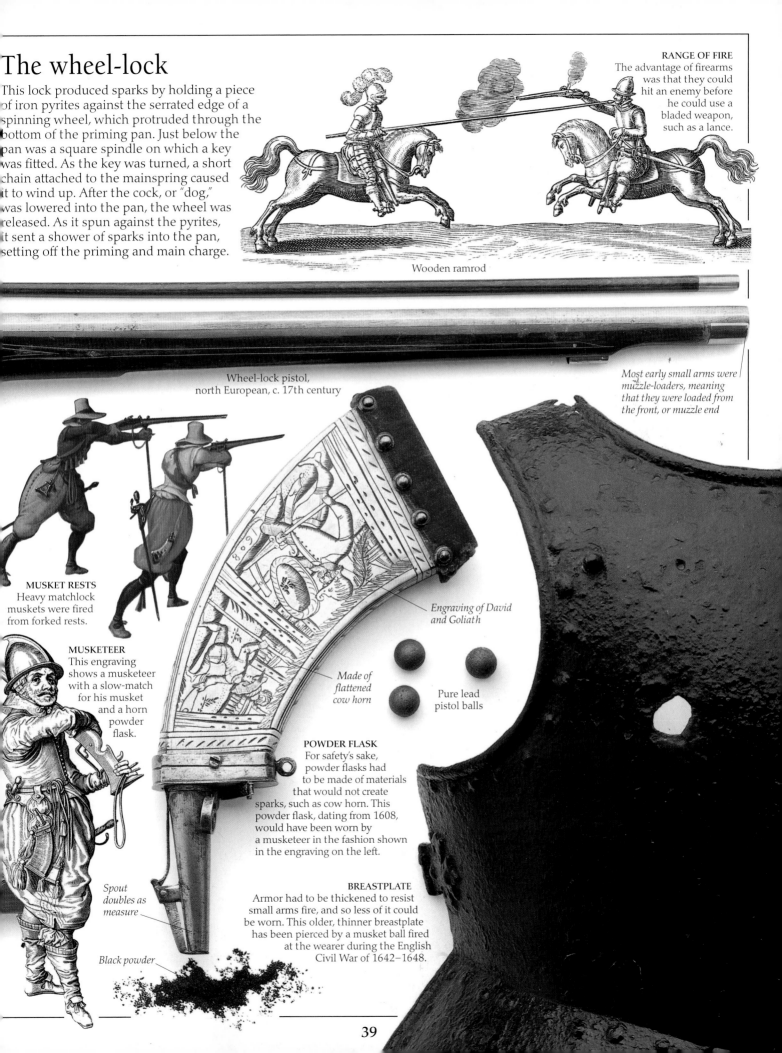

RANGE OF FIRE
The advantage of firearms was that they could hit an enemy before he could use a bladed weapon, such as a lance.

Wooden ramrod

Wheel-lock pistol, north European, c. 17th century

Most early small arms were muzzle-loaders, meaning that they were loaded from the front, or muzzle end

MUSKET RESTS
Heavy matchlock muskets were fired from forked rests.

MUSKETEER
This engraving shows a musketeer with a slow-match for his musket and a horn powder flask.

Engraving of David and Goliath

Made of flattened cow horn

Pure lead pistol balls

POWDER FLASK
For safety's sake, powder flasks had to be made of materials that would not create sparks, such as cow horn. This powder flask, dating from 1608, would have been worn by a musketeer in the fashion shown in the engraving on the left.

Spout doubles as measure

BREASTPLATE
Armor had to be thickened to resist small arms fire, and so less of it could be worn. This older, thinner breastplate has been pierced by a musket ball fired at the wearer during the English Civil War of 1642–1648.

Black powder

Flintlock firearms

MORE RELIABLE THAN THE MATCHLOCK and cheaper than the wheel-lock (pp. 38–39), flintlock ignition was used on most European and American firearms from the late 17th century until the 1840s. Probably invented in France by Martin Le Bourgeoys in the 1620s, the flintlock mechanism could be set in two positions— one for firing and one for safety. With its basic design improved only by a few details, the flintlock ignition dominated the battlefields in all the major wars of the period. It also became an important civilian weapon, used for dueling (pp. 46–47), self-defense (pp. 48–49), and shooting game, with many of these firearms showing the highest standards of craftsmanship.

The pirate Long John Silver in Robert Louis Stevenson's *Treasure Island*

SPORTSMAN SHOOTING GAME
As this hunter fires his flintlock "fowling piece," the flash from the pan can be clearly seen.

Loading a flintlock

First, the lock was set to the "half-cock" safety position. Using a powder flask (p. 39) or a torn-open cartridge (left), a small amount of powder was poured into the priming pan. After closing the pan cover, the correct amount of powder for the main charge was poured down the barrel from the flask or cartridge. Then the ball, either wrapped in its patch (p. 46) or along with the screwed-up cartridge paper, was rammed down the barrel with the ramrod. Once the lock had been set to the "full-cock" position, the flintlock was ready to fire.

Musket ball

MUSKET CARTRIDGE POUCH
Each paper cartridge contains powder and ball for one shot.

Lock

Pan cover

Priming pan

Brass butt-cap

Brown walnut stock

Socket

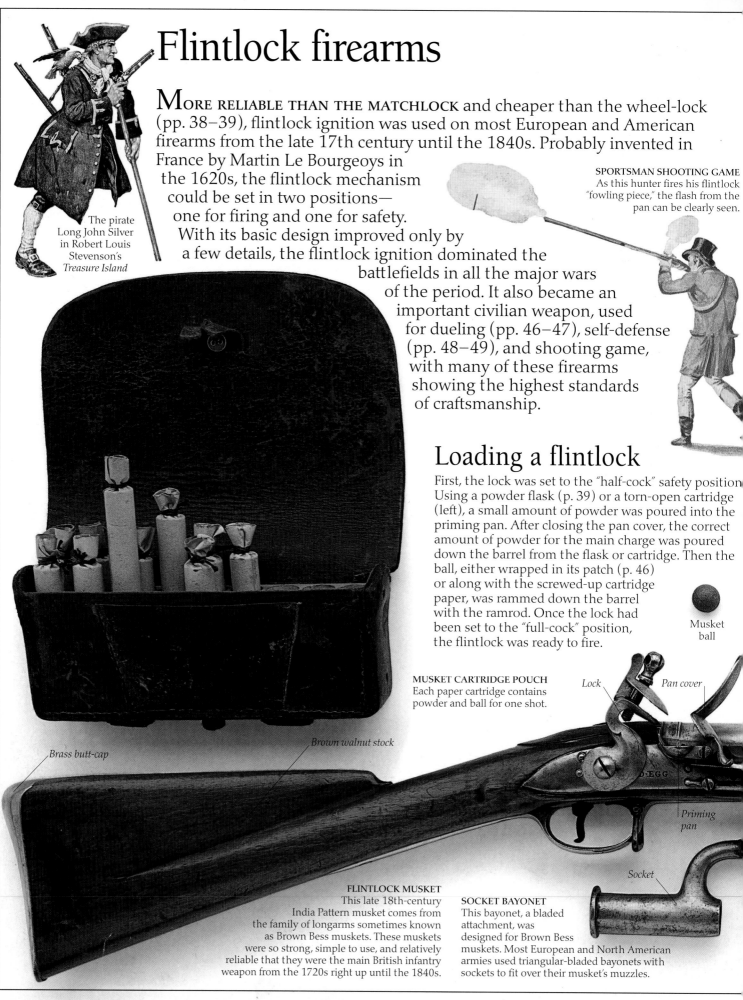

FLINTLOCK MUSKET
This late 18th-century India Pattern musket comes from the family of longarms sometimes known as Brown Bess muskets. These muskets were so strong, simple to use, and relatively reliable that they were the main British infantry weapon from the 1720s right up until the 1840s.

SOCKET BAYONET
This bayonet, a bladed attachment, was designed for Brown Bess muskets. Most European and North American armies used triangular-bladed bayonets with sockets to fit over their musket's muzzles.

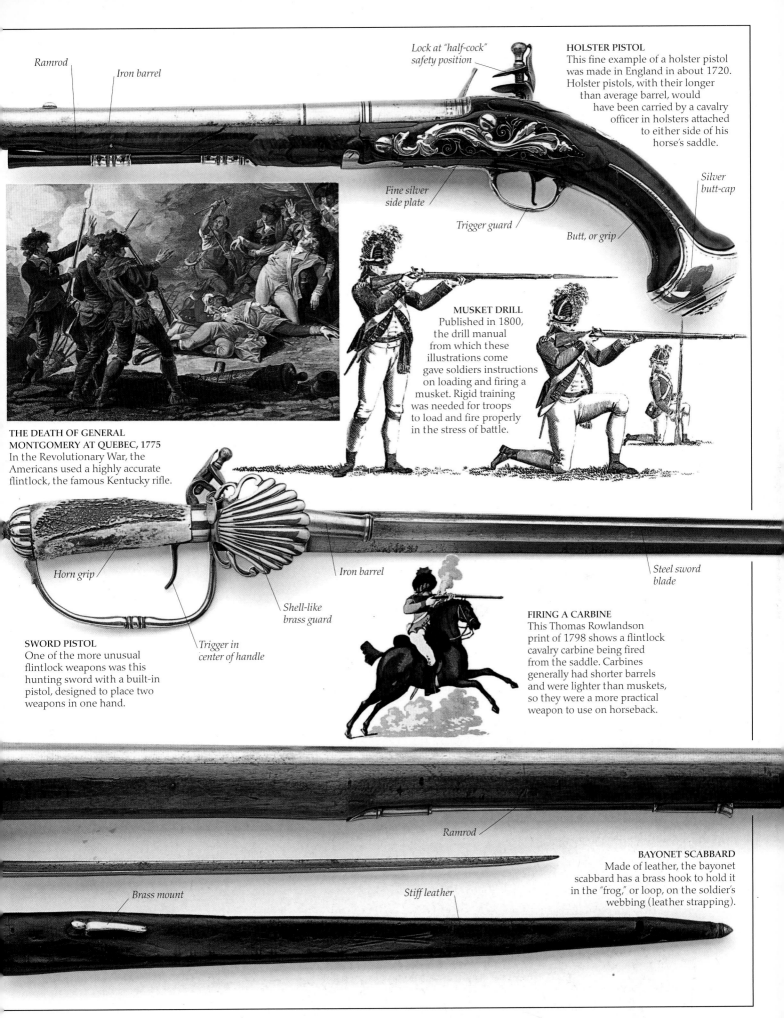

Ramrod

Iron barrel

Lock at "half-cock" safety position

HOLSTER PISTOL
This fine example of a holster pistol was made in England in about 1720. Holster pistols, with their longer than average barrel, would have been carried by a cavalry officer in holsters attached to either side of his horse's saddle.

Fine silver side plate

Silver butt-cap

Trigger guard

Butt, or grip

THE DEATH OF GENERAL MONTGOMERY AT QUEBEC, 1775
In the Revolutionary War, the Americans used a highly accurate flintlock, the famous Kentucky rifle.

MUSKET DRILL
Published in 1800, the drill manual from which these illustrations come gave soldiers instructions on loading and firing a musket. Rigid training was needed for troops to load and fire properly in the stress of battle.

Horn grip

Iron barrel

Steel sword blade

Shell-like brass guard

SWORD PISTOL
One of the more unusual flintlock weapons was this hunting sword with a built-in pistol, designed to place two weapons in one hand.

Trigger in center of handle

FIRING A CARBINE
This Thomas Rowlandson print of 1798 shows a flintlock cavalry carbine being fired from the saddle. Carbines generally had shorter barrels and were lighter than muskets, so they were a more practical weapon to use on horseback.

Ramrod

BAYONET SCABBARD
Made of leather, the bayonet scabbard has a brass hook to hold it in the "frog," or loop, on the soldier's webbing (leather strapping).

Brass mount

Stiff leather

Dueling swords

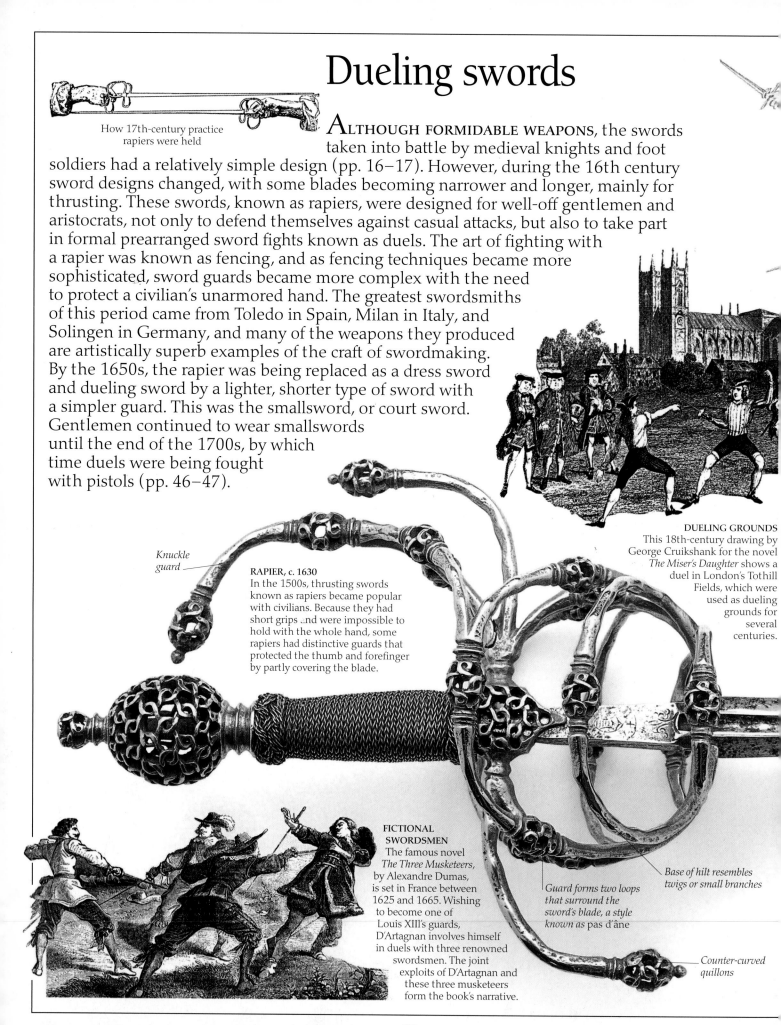

How 17th-century practice rapiers were held

ALTHOUGH FORMIDABLE WEAPONS, the swords taken into battle by medieval knights and foot soldiers had a relatively simple design (pp. 16–17). However, during the 16th century sword designs changed, with some blades becoming narrower and longer, mainly for thrusting. These swords, known as rapiers, were designed for well-off gentlemen and aristocrats, not only to defend themselves against casual attacks, but also to take part in formal prearranged sword fights known as duels. The art of fighting with a rapier was known as fencing, and as fencing techniques became more sophisticated, sword guards became more complex with the need to protect a civilian's unarmored hand. The greatest swordsmiths of this period came from Toledo in Spain, Milan in Italy, and Solingen in Germany, and many of the weapons they produced are artistically superb examples of the craft of swordmaking. By the 1650s, the rapier was being replaced as a dress sword and dueling sword by a lighter, shorter type of sword with a simpler guard. This was the smallsword, or court sword. Gentlemen continued to wear smallswords until the end of the 1700s, by which time duels were being fought with pistols (pp. 46–47).

DUELING GROUNDS
This 18th-century drawing by George Cruikshank for the novel *The Miser's Daughter* shows a duel in London's Tothill Fields, which were used as dueling grounds for several centuries.

Knuckle guard

RAPIER, c. 1630
In the 1500s, thrusting swords known as rapiers became popular with civilians. Because they had short grips and were impossible to hold with the whole hand, some rapiers had distinctive guards that protected the thumb and forefinger by partly covering the blade.

FICTIONAL SWORDSMEN
The famous novel *The Three Musketeers*, by Alexandre Dumas, is set in France between 1625 and 1665. Wishing to become one of Louis XIII's guards, D'Artagnan involves himself in duels with three renowned swordsmen. The joint exploits of D'Artagnan and these three musketeers form the book's narrative.

Guard forms two loops that surround the sword's blade, a style known as pas d'âne

Base of hilt resembles twigs or small branches

Counter-curved quillons

PARRYING WITH A DAGGER
Fencing—the art of fighting with a rapier—was developed principally in France and Italy in the early 1600s. This engraving by Jacques Callot is of a fencer practicing with a left-handed parrying dagger.

SMALLSWORD, c. 1740
In the early 17th century, the rapier began to be replaced by a lighter sword with a simpler hilt. Made in France, this smallsword would have been used both for dueling and as an item of everyday dress.

Simple hilt with a shell-shaped guard made of chiseled steel and partly gilt

Straight, double-edged blade

Grip is short, so thumb extended onto blade through this hole

PARRYING DAGGER, c. 1650 *left*
This dagger for parrying an opponent's blow in dueling was misleadingly called a *main gauche* (French for left hand), even though it could be held in either hand.

Long, thin, double-edged blade

SABER EXERCISES
A saber, with its slightly curved, single-edged blade, was used mainly for cutting, but it was also effective as a thrusting weapon. These three illustrations showing military exercises on foot come from an early 19th-century handkerchief.

SIX SABER CUTS
This face on the handkerchief of saber sword exercises (above) shows the directions of the six cuts that could be aimed at an opponent's head.

Light, triangular-sectioned thrusting blade

FENCING MOVE, c. 1640 *below*
The swordsman on the right, using a rapier and parrying dagger, passes his adversary and disengages under his dagger, thus killing him.

A CELEBRATED FRENCH DUEL *right*
This 19th-century engraving depicts a duel fought in Paris, France, in 1578. It involved Henri III's favorite, Quèlus. The duelists' seconds also became involved, and by the end of the duel, three men had received fatal wounds, including Quèlus.

43

Continued on next page

PRUSSIAN HUSSARS
The hussar on the right is carrying the type of saber that had become the main edged weapon of European light cavalry by the beginning of the 19th century.

SWORDSMITH'S SHOP, c. 1755
In a Parisian swordsmith's shop, a customer is testing a new blade, while workmen near the window are making sword hilts.

BACKSWORD, c. 1620
A backsword was a type of military sword used by European cavalry in the 17th century for both cutting and thrusting at an opponent in battle.

Guard for protecting the hand, similar to the guard of a rapier

Blade of 17th-century parrying dagger (p. 43)

Blade of 17th-century rapier (pp. 42–43)

THE BATTLE OF DENAIN
In this painting of a battle fought in 1712 between the French and an Anglo–Dutch army, the French victor, Marechal de Villars, uses his smallsword to rally his men.

These heads were said to refer to the executed King Charles I, so in England broadswords with this decoration were called "mortuary" swords

Bars completely protected the hand

Running wolf engraving, originally used by well-known German blade-makers

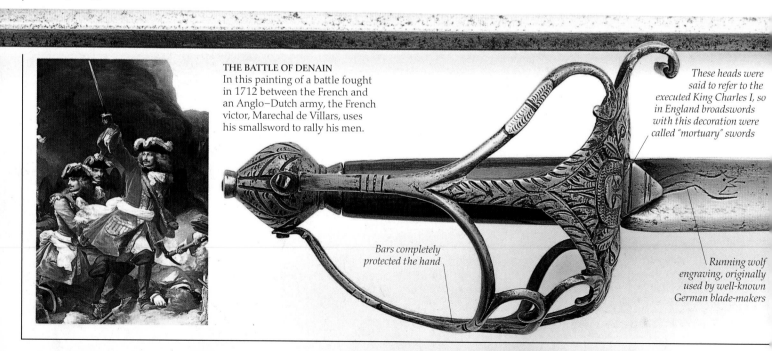

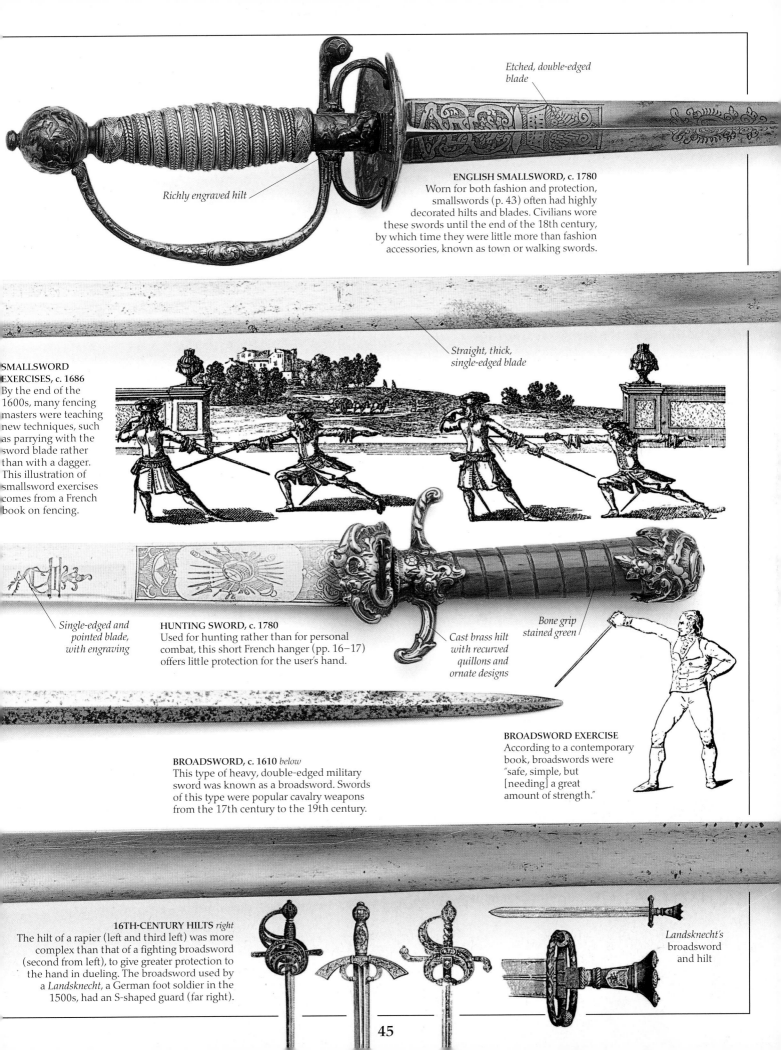

ENGLISH SMALLSWORD, c. 1780
Worn for both fashion and protection, smallswords (p. 43) often had highly decorated hilts and blades. Civilians wore these swords until the end of the 18th century, by which time they were little more than fashion accessories, known as town or walking swords.

Etched, double-edged blade

Richly engraved hilt

SMALLSWORD EXERCISES, c. 1686
By the end of the 1600s, many fencing masters were teaching new techniques, such as parrying with the sword blade rather than with a dagger. This illustration of smallsword exercises comes from a French book on fencing.

Straight, thick, single-edged blade

Single-edged and pointed blade, with engraving

HUNTING SWORD, c. 1780
Used for hunting rather than for personal combat, this short French hanger (pp. 16–17) offers little protection for the user's hand.

Cast brass hilt with recurved quillons and ornate designs

Bone grip stained green

BROADSWORD EXERCISE
According to a contemporary book, broadswords were "safe, simple, but [needing] a great amount of strength."

BROADSWORD, c. 1610 *below*
This type of heavy, double-edged military sword was known as a broadsword. Swords of this type were popular cavalry weapons from the 17th century to the 19th century.

16TH-CENTURY HILTS *right*
The hilt of a rapier (left and third left) was more complex than that of a fighting broadsword (second from left), to give greater protection to the hand in dueling. The broadsword used by a *Landsknecht*, a German foot soldier in the 1500s, had an S-shaped guard (far right).

Landsknecht's broadsword and hilt

Dueling pistols

Aᴌᴛʜᴏᴜɢʜ ɪʟʟᴇɢᴀʟ, for centuries dueling was a popular way for "gentlemen" and army officers to settle their quarrels. By the late 18th century, flintlock pistols had replaced swords (pp. 42–45) as the preferred weapons for fighting a duel. Gunsmiths began to make special dueling pistols in matched pairs, which they supplied in a case that also contained all the necessary accessories for both making the bullets and cleaning and loading the pistols. In order that dueling pistols should be as accurate as possible, the pistols were of the highest quality, with added refinement such as sights and special triggers. Dueling pistols were muzzle-loaders (pp. 38–39), and all used flintlock ignition until around 1820 to 1830.

Spring-loaded trigger

SENSITIVE TRIGGER
Many dueling pistols had a special hair- or set-trigger, worked by an extra spring in the lock. These light triggers allowed the user to fire the pistol without disturbing his aim.

Butt—rear part of stock

Wooden end for holding ramrod

Grip—part of stock where pistol is held

WOODEN STOCK
In all dueling pistols, the wooden stock was carefully made so that the butt would fit comfortably in the duelist's hand. Some pistols had a squarer, saw-handled butt to assist the grip.

Making a bullet

The bullet, or lead ball, was made at home by the firer, using a bullet mold provided with the pistol. Lead was melted over a fire and poured into the mold. After a few seconds, the scissorlike mold was opened and the ball shaken out. Excess lead, or sprue, was cut off with the shears incorporated into the mold handles.

Lead-ball bullets

Black gunpowder

LINEN PATCH
To fit tightly in the barrel, the bullet was wrapped in a cloth or leather patch.

ALEKSANDR PUSHKIN
Eminent men who took part in duels included the British general and statesman the Duke of Wellington, and the French politician Georges Clemenceau. A famous victim was the Russian writer Pushkin (below), killed in a duel with his wife's lover in 1837.

Nozzle forms a measure

RAMROD
A wood or metal ramrod (kept in a recess below the barrel) was used to push the ball and patch down the bore. Many ramrods had attachments for cleaning out the bore.

Hollow chamber

BULLET MOLD
Bullets were made by pouring molten lead into the hollow chamber of the bullet mold (p. 57).

POWDER FLASK
Gunpowder was kept in a powder flask. Originally made of wood or horn (p. 39), by the 19th century most powder flasks were made of metal. When self-contained cartridges were introduced, powder flasks became obsolete.

Metal end for ramming bullet down bore

AMERICAN ANTI-DUELING CARTOON, c. 1821
When this anti-dueling cartoon was published in Philadelphia, dueling was as popular in the United States as it was in countries such as France and England.

AN AFFAIR OF HONOR, c. 1820
Duels were called "affairs of honor." A gentleman who considered himself insulted by the behavior of another would challenge him to a duel. To refuse to be "called out" cast a bad slur on a gentleman's honor. Robert Cruikshank painted this fatal duel at the height of the dueling era.

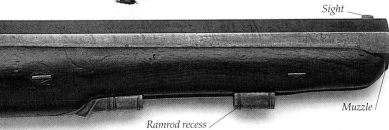

Sight

Muzzle

Ramrod recess

BARREL
Dueling pistols were muzzle-loaders (pp. 38–39). The outside of the barrel was usually octagonal in shape and equipped with sights.

Pair of English dueling pistols, c. 1800 (lock of lower pistol shown separately)

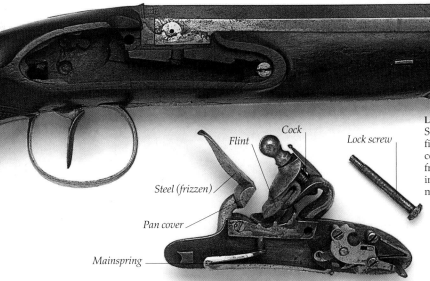

Cock

Flint

Lock screw

Steel (frizzen)

Pan cover

Mainspring

LOCK *left*
Screwed to the side of the stock was the lock—the mechanism that fired the pistol. When the trigger of a flintlock was pulled, the cock swung forward, making sparks by scraping the flint down the frizzen, or steel, and pushing open the pan cover. The sparks fell into the priming powder, which burned with a flash and set off the main powder charge in the barrel, through the small "touch-hole."

THE RULES OF DUELING
In pistol duels, combatants had to follow a strict set of rules. The rules of the fight were agreed upon by the two men and their "seconds"—friends who loaded the pistols and witnessed the duel. Usually, the two duelists stood an agreed upon number of paces apart, with their pistols pointing at the ground. At a given signal, such as the dropping of a handkerchief by one of the seconds, the duelists raised their pistols and fired.

Cleaning a flintlock

First, any unfired ball and powder was removed from the barrel with a tool that was attached to the ramrod or a special cleaning rod. Then the empty barrel was oiled using a cloth fixed to the end of the rod. After brushing away burned gunpowder from in and around the priming pan, the lock was oiled and the flint was replaced if worn out.

Oil can for oiling lock and barrel

A nonfatal duel, fought in France in 1893

PAN BRUSH
The priming pan needed frequent cleaning.

FLINTS AND LEATHERS
Leather was used to grip the flint in the jaws of the lock.

Spare flints

TURNSCREW
A turnscrew was used for removing the lock.

Attack by highwaymen

In the lawless days before guns were subject to licensing, many firearms were made or adapted for self-defense against armed robbers, either on the road or in the home. A gentleman on horseback could carry a pair of holster pistols on his saddle. When traveling by coach he could keep a small pistol in his coat pocket, or he or the coach's guard could carry a blunderbuss. The blunderbuss, named after the Dutch word for "thunder gun," was well suited to close-range confrontations, and it was used to defend ships as well as travelers. The gun's wide muzzle helped to intimidate opponents and if that failed to deter its charge of numerous lead balls gave the owner a better chance of hitting the target. Blunderbusses were often equipped with spring bayonets for extra protection, while pistol butts could be used as clubs. Inevitably, such weapons proved equally useful to the highwaymen.

FOOTPAD AMBUSH
This 1813 cartoon by Thomas Rowlandson shows a gentleman being held up by three armed footpads—robbers who traveled on foot.

Flintlock mechanism (some parts missing)

FLINTLOCK BLUNDERBUSS
Blunderbusses fired a charge of small lead balls called shot for close-range effect. This late 18th-century blunderbuss has a spring-loaded bayonet. On releasing the catch, the bayonet would flip forward and lock in position.

Ramrod

Flintlock mechanism

Two brass barrels set side-by-side

POCKET PISTOL
With a double-barreled pistol, both barrels were fired by the same lock. The iron slider on the boxlike frame selected which barrel was connected with the flash pan. This particular pocket pistol was made in London in around 1785.

Iron slider for switching barrels

Butt-cap

Partially opened spring bayonet

Bayonet spring and lock

Brass barrel

Bayonet catch

Ramrod

DICK TURPIN *left*
During the 1730s, Dick Turpin, the legendary highwayman, was the most wanted man in England. Here, Turpin is shown improbably firing two pistols in opposite directions, while jumping a tollgate on his famous horse Black Bess.

TRICORNE HAT
A tricorne, or three-cornered, hat would have been worn by the more well-to-do 18th-century highwaymen.

ROBERT MACAIRE
During the 18th century, celebrated highwaymen often became folk heroes. Here, a notorious robber named Robert Macaire is being portrayed by an actor named Mr. Hicks.

HOLSTER PISTOL
The butt-cap of this early 18th-century holster pistol allowed the pistol to be reversed and used as a club once the single shot had been fired.

Butt-cap

AN ATTACK BY HIGHWAYMEN
In 1750, two highwaymen robbed Lord Eglinton, who was riding in his post-chaise carriage near London. On this occasion, the blunderbuss his lordship is shown holding proved useless.

Bizarre hand weapons

THROUGHOUT recorded history, many extraordinary and seemingly impractical weapons have been made alongside more conventional swords, guns, and bows and arrows. The unusual examples shown on these pages prove that many local and tribal weapons were just as ingenious and deadly as the specialized weapons devised for close-range attack and defense, or the strange-looking combination pistols made by gunsmiths for their rich customers.

Hand-shaped head of mace

ITALIAN GUNNER'S STILETTO *below*
The engraving on the blade of this 18th-century dagger is a numbered scale for artillery commanders to calculate the bore size of cannons.

Engraved blade

ANTIPERSONNEL DEVICE *left*
Caltrops, also called crow's feet, were ancient weapons made of sharp iron spikes. They were strewn in front of infantrymen's feet and horses' hooves.

Curved blade with single edge

Dagger blade

THE LAST ARMOR *below*
In the 1700s and 1800s, the only piece of armor regularly worn by European or American infantry was the gorget (p. 26), worn as a mark of rank for officers rather than for defense. Today, gorgets are still used with full dress in some countries. The gorget below belonged to an officer of the marines in the British navy, in around 1800.

Gorget

Trigger

Barrel concealed in brass handle

Muzzle plug was removed before firing

CUTLERY PISTOLS *right*
Among the most impractical flintlock firearms ever devised must be this companion knife and fork, made in Germany in about 1740.

GURKHA KNIFE
The *kukri* is the national knife and principal weapon of the Gurkhas of Nepal. While the *kukri* is useful for cutting through thick jungle, its heavy, curved blade also makes it a deadly fighting weapon.

INDIAN MACE
This all-steel mace was made in India in the 19th century. Although the owner would have used the mace to lean on while he was sitting down, he would still have been able to club any possible assailant with its hand-shaped metal head.

APACHE PISTOL *right*
In around 1900, a gang of criminals in Paris, France, called themselves Apaches, after the warlike North American tribe of the same name. The gang used specially made pinfire revolvers that had a folding blade and brass-knuckle butt.

No barrel, so pistol could only be fired at point-blank range

Six chambers

End of grip was inserted into musket muzzle

Folding dagger

Folding trigger

Brass-knuckle butt

Numbered scale on flat of blade

Sharp point for thrusting

Ornate ivory grip

BOY'S SWORD *below*
In the 18th century, wealthy parents gave small swords to their sons when they left the nursery.

Miniature version of classic smallsword (pp. 44–45)

Scroll handle ending in a lotus flower

PLUG BAYONET
First used in around 1650, early bayonets were sharp blades that were inserted into the muzzle of a musket for use as a secondary weapon. Plug bayonets were replaced by socket bayonets (p. 40) in about 1700.

Made of wrought steel

Originally screwed into a short stick that concealed the blade, making it harmless to lean upon

WAR FLAIL *left*
This medieval weapon was used against armor. It consisted of a bar connected by a swivel to a haft, or one or more balls linked by a chain, all often studded with spikes.

INDIAN STEEL DAGGER
This Indian dagger formed part of a weapon used by fakirs, or Hindu holy men. The complete weapon, called a fakir's crutch, consisted of a dagger concealed in a steel stick on which the fakir could lean when seated.

FAKIR'S HORNS
This unusual-looking Indian weapon, known as fakir's horns, is a double-ended dagger with horn grips. It was used as a defensive weapon by the Hindu holy men called fakirs, who were not allowed to carry conventional weapons.

Steel spikes on end of horns

Blackbuck horns

Lion's-head pommel

MIDSHIPMAN'S DIRK *below*
Called a dirk, this type of hanger (pp. 16–17) was worn by young naval officers in the 19th century. Since each officer had his own weapon specially made before he joined his ship, these weapons are often highly individualistic.

Ivory grip

Single-edged, curved blade

Grenadiers and cavalry

FRENCH GRENADIER
Despite his title of grenadier, the main weapon of this soldier in the French Light Infantry was his flintlock musket.

GRENADIER'S POUCH AND BELT
This 18th-century English grenadier's pouch is decorated with a one-legged grenadier. Grenadiers of this period wore special pointed caps to enable them to throw grenades overarm.

Brass match case

Brush to remove excess gunpowder

BY THE TIME Napoleon Bonaparte was conquering most of Europe, at the beginning of the 1800s, flintlock firearms—muskets, carbines, and pistols—had become the chief weapons of armies in both Europe and North America (pp. 40–41). Among the specialized flintlocks were grenade-launchers—weapons for destroying defensive works, such as doorways and barricades. Originally, grenades were used by specially trained troops called grenadiers. But by the 19th century, most so-called grenadiers were ordinary infantry troops who used flintlock muskets rather than grenades. In the Napoleonic wars, muskets proved such formidable weapons that they often destroyed the effectiveness of mounted troops, who relied more on swords and lances than on firearms.

Iron case

Charge hole

Fuse

Early hand grenade

Velvet pouch

Grenade

Grenade pouch

Lighted match

Gunstock

British army pattern grenade-launcher, late 18th century

Weapon weighs 11 lb (5 kg)

Live grenade

Single-edged blade

Buff leather belt

SOLDIER LIGHTING GRENADE *left*
By the late 1600s, small bombs known as hand grenades were commonly used in European battles. Early grenades were hollow iron balls filled with black gunpowder. Holes were bored through the wall of the grenade (see opposite page, centre) and threaded with a short fuse.

GRENADE LAUNCHER
This formidable-looking weapon was designed to increase the range of grenades, which were fired from its wide barrel. Any miscalculation over the lighting of the grenade fuse was liable to cause fatal injuries to the grenadier and anyone nearby.

Broad barrel to accommodate grenade

Fleur-de-lys

CAVALRY SWORD
This 18th-century French saber has a brass hilt decorated with a fleur-de-lys, the royal emblem of France. The sword has a single-edged, straight blade.

Engraving reads Pro Deo fide et Patria— *"For God, Faith, and Country"*

CAVALRY CHARGE *below*
At the Battle of Waterloo in 1815, the British infantry formed squares four ranks deep to face the French cavalry charges. While one rank of a square fired a volley, other ranks reloaded. The French cavalry's inability to penetrate the "hedge" of bayonets presented by the squares proved decisive in the battle.

British militia officer's shako, c. 1840

Basket-shaped hilt protects the entire hand

Napoleon Bonaparte in 1812

FRENCH CUIRASSIER'S SABER
The cuirassier, or heavy cavalry, regiments in Napoleon's army used sabers like this, with a slightly curved blade and a gilded brass hilt.

OFFICER'S SHAKO
In the 1800s, stiff, peaked caps called shakos were worn in many armies (see also opposite page, top left).

Keeping law and order

SINCE THE WORD "POLICE" MEANS different types of forces in different countries—civilian and military, uniformed and plain-clothed—the nightsticks, rattles, and other law-enforcement equipment shown on these pages are best described as weapons for combatting crime and keeping public order. All of them were in use during the 19th century, and when it is considered how much violent crime and civilian unrest took place at that time, such weapons seem hardly sufficent. Of course, more powerful weapons were issued to some police forces out of necessity. By the late 19th century, the Berlin police force was armed with swords, pistols, and brass knuckles, while the police in the US cities of New York and Boston first used firearms in the 1850s. However, in most European and American towns, the increasing respect felt for the ordinary civilian law-enforcement officer was due in part to his being so lightly armed.

POLICE SWORD
Short swords were issued to 19th-century police forces and prison guards in Britain. Although they were not standard equipment, they were kept in police stations and prisons for use in riots and emergency situations.

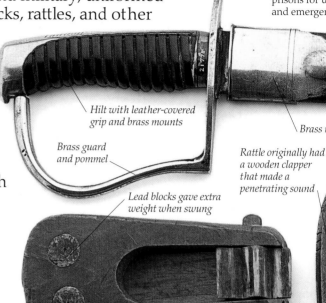

Hilt with leather-covered grip and brass mounts

Brass guard and pommel

Brass mount

Rattle originally had a wooden clapper that made a penetrating sound

Lead blocks gave extra weight when swung

POLICE RATTLES
Lead blocks in a rattle (above) made it a useful weapon, in addition to giving it extra weight when it was swung. Rattles with clappers (right) made an especially loud noise.

Buckle for securing at the back of the neck

LEATHER COLLAR
In some early police forces, officers wore leather collars called stocks to protect them from being garotted—strangled with a cord. Stocks were hot to wear and also restricted movement.

Twin handles

Outer tin shell

CARTOON POLICEMAN
In the 19th century, images of policemen were often used to frighten children into behaving well, as can be seen from this illustration of a policeman in a child's gift book dating from 1867.

Stock is 4 in (10 cm) wide

Ground glass magnifying lens

BULLS-EYE LANTERN
The standard British police lamp in the 19th century, the bulls-eye lantern hooked onto the belt that the policeman wore over his overcoat.

POLICE WHISTLE
Whistles were adopted by many police forces during the 19th century, since they could be heard over far greater distances than the sound from a rattle.

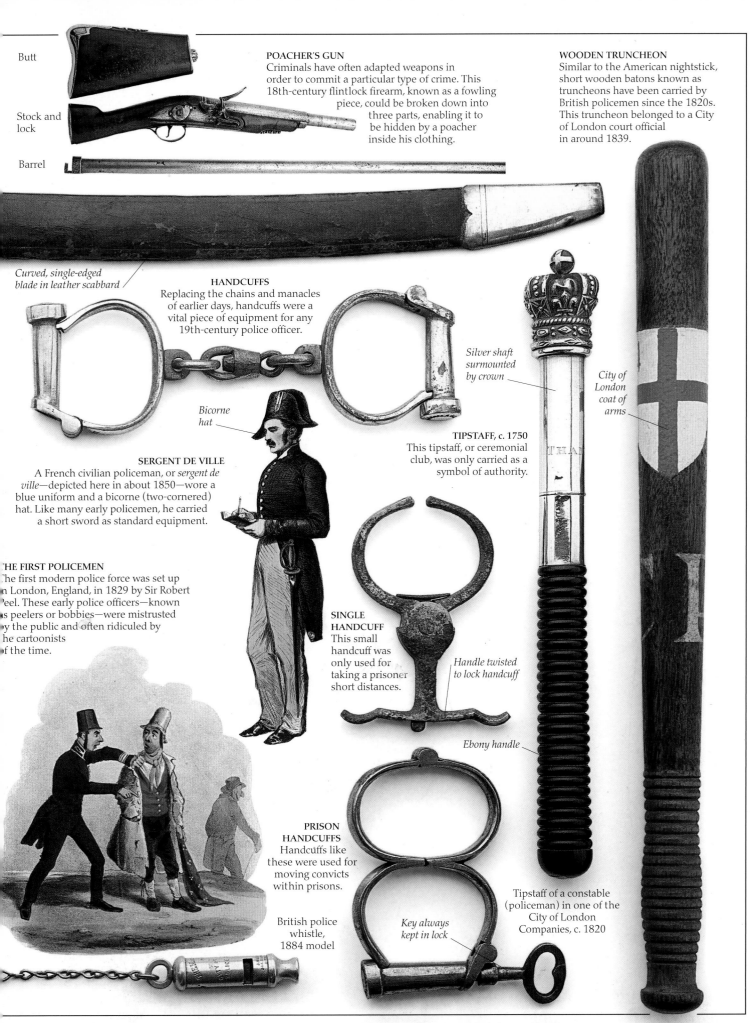

Butt

Stock and lock

Barrel

POACHER'S GUN
Criminals have often adapted weapons in order to commit a particular type of crime. This 18th-century flintlock firearm, known as a fowling piece, could be broken down into three parts, enabling it to be hidden by a poacher inside his clothing.

WOODEN TRUNCHEON
Similar to the American nightstick, short wooden batons known as truncheons have been carried by British policemen since the 1820s. This truncheon belonged to a City of London court official in around 1839.

Curved, single-edged blade in leather scabbard

HANDCUFFS
Replacing the chains and manacles of earlier days, handcuffs were a vital piece of equipment for any 19th-century police officer.

Silver shaft surmounted by crown

City of London coat of arms

Bicorne hat

SERGENT DE VILLE
A French civilian policeman, or *sergent de ville*—depicted here in about 1850—wore a blue uniform and a bicorne (two-cornered) hat. Like many early policemen, he carried a short sword as standard equipment.

TIPSTAFF, c. 1750
This tipstaff, or ceremonial club, was only carried as a symbol of authority.

THE FIRST POLICEMEN
The first modern police force was set up in London, England, in 1829 by Sir Robert Peel. These early police officers—known as peelers or bobbies—were mistrusted by the public and often ridiculed by the cartoonists of the time.

SINGLE HANDCUFF
This small handcuff was only used for taking a prisoner short distances.

Handle twisted to lock handcuff

Ebony handle

PRISON HANDCUFFS
Handcuffs like these were used for moving convicts within prisons.

British police whistle, 1884 model

Key always kept in lock

Tipstaff of a constable (policeman) in one of the City of London Companies, c. 1820

55

Pistols

A **PISTOL IS SIMPLY** a short-barreled firearm designed to be used with one hand—a convenient weapon to carry, but one that needs a lot of practice to fire accurately. During the 19th century, a great variety of pistols were designed for both military and civilian use. Some could fire only a single shot, but others, called revolvers, could fire a succession of shots before they needed to be reloaded.

OPEN CYLINDER
The open cylinder of a Colt revolver is shown here at the moment when the empty cartridge cases are ejected, before reloading.

One of three bands for holding barrel in stock

COSSACK PISTOL
From the Caucasus in southern Russia, this pistol has a miquelet lock—a type of flintlock used mainly in Spain and the Middle East. The Cossacks used similar pistols to this in the 18th and 19th centuries.

ASSASSIN'S PISTOL *below*
This unusual revolver, known as a palm pistol or "lemon squeezer," was held almost hidden in the hand and fired with a squeezing action. One was used to assassinate President William McKinley in 1901.

"BUNTLINE SPECIAL" REVOLVER *above*
This long-barreled version of the Colt Peacemaker (p. 61) was made famous by the 19th-century American writer Ned Buntline, author of more than 400 action novels.

Hammer

TRANSITIONAL REVOLVER *above*
Representing an intermediate stage between the pepperbox and the true revolver, this weapon was cheap and popular during the 1850s.

Seven-shot cylinder

Barrel

Hammer

Six barrels

Trigger rotates the barrel and fires the shot

PEPPERBOX REVOLVER
The front-loading pepperbox was an early form of revolver with a cluster of barrels, the muzzles of which resembled the holes in a pepperpot. Pepperboxes were popular between 1830 and 1860, despite their unreliability.

Bullet mold for combination pistol

Folding dagger blade

Pistol barrel

COMBINATION PISTOL
A popular weapon of the 1840s and 1850s was the combined pistol and pocketknife. This example includes a pistol, two knife blades, a ramrod, and space in the grip for ammunition.

Folding pocketknife blade

Folding trigger

Hollow grip for ammunition and bullet mold

Decorated brasswork

Ramrod

Barrel is 12 in (305 mm) long

POCKET, OR MUFF, PISTOL
This percussion pistol (pp. 58–59) of about 1850 was kept in a man's pocket or a lady's winter muff. Its trigger folded into the pistol when not in use.

A .36-caliber cartridge for Colt Police Revolver

COLT POLICE REVOLVER *above*
Among the many types of pistol produced by Colt from the 1830s onward was the Model 1862 Police Revolver, a front-loading, five-shot gun.

Gun loaded through side gate

anyard ring r cord so at pistol can ng around e neck or oulder

Ejector rod to knock out empty cartridge cases

PINFIRE CARTRIDGE
The pistol's hammer struck the brass pin, which set off a detonator inside the cartridge.

FRENCH PINFIRE REVOLVER
Pinfire weapons were among the first to use a self-contained cartridge in which bullet, powder, and cap were all held in a brass case. The cartridge could be loaded quickly from the breech (rear) end, and its case stopped the explosion from leaking back toward the firer's hand. This 1855 revolver is the work of the famous French gunsmith Casimir Lefaucheux, inventor of the pinfire cartridge.

Two barrels

"OVER-AND-UNDER" PISTOL
Made in around 1820, this English pocket pistol has two barrels, one above the other. Each has its own flintlock mechanism, but a clever design allows both barrels to be fired by just one trigger.

Single trigger

Percussion firearms

HUNTING WAS THE MAIN IMPETUS for the development of percussion ignition. The flash and smoke from the flint in the priming pan often gave brief warning to an animal before the main charge went off. But percussion, introduced in the 19th century, provided instantaneous ignition and better resistance to wet weather. Typically, a thimble-cap containing detonating compound was placed on a steel nipple. The cap exploded when struck by the weapon's hammer, sending a jet of flame through the nipple into the main charge. Early percussion guns were still muzzle-loaders (pp. 38–39), with the cap separate from the powder and ball. Later, the cap, powder, and ball were all incorporated into a metallic cartridge. The metal case sealed in the explosive gases, enabling efficient breech- (rear-) loading firearms to be produced.

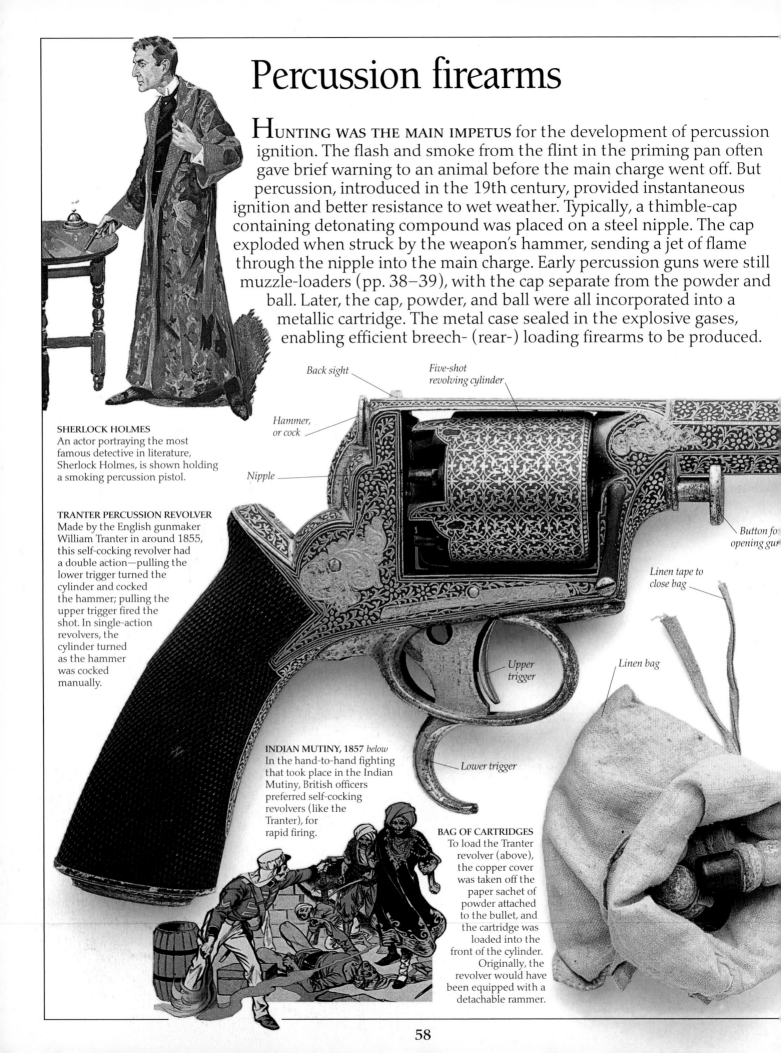

SHERLOCK HOLMES
An actor portraying the most famous detective in literature, Sherlock Holmes, is shown holding a smoking percussion pistol.

TRANTER PERCUSSION REVOLVER
Made by the English gunmaker William Tranter in around 1855, this self-cocking revolver had a double action—pulling the lower trigger turned the cylinder and cocked the hammer; pulling the upper trigger fired the shot. In single-action revolvers, the cylinder turned as the hammer was cocked manually.

INDIAN MUTINY, 1857 *below*
In the hand-to-hand fighting that took place in the Indian Mutiny, British officers preferred self-cocking revolvers (like the Tranter), for rapid firing.

BAG OF CARTRIDGES
To load the Tranter revolver (above), the copper cover was taken off the paper sachet of powder attached to the bullet, and the cartridge was loaded into the front of the cylinder. Originally, the revolver would have been equipped with a detachable rammer.

Back sight

Five-shot revolving cylinder

Hammer, or cock

Nipple

Button for opening gun

Linen tape to close bag

Linen bag

Upper trigger

Lower trigger

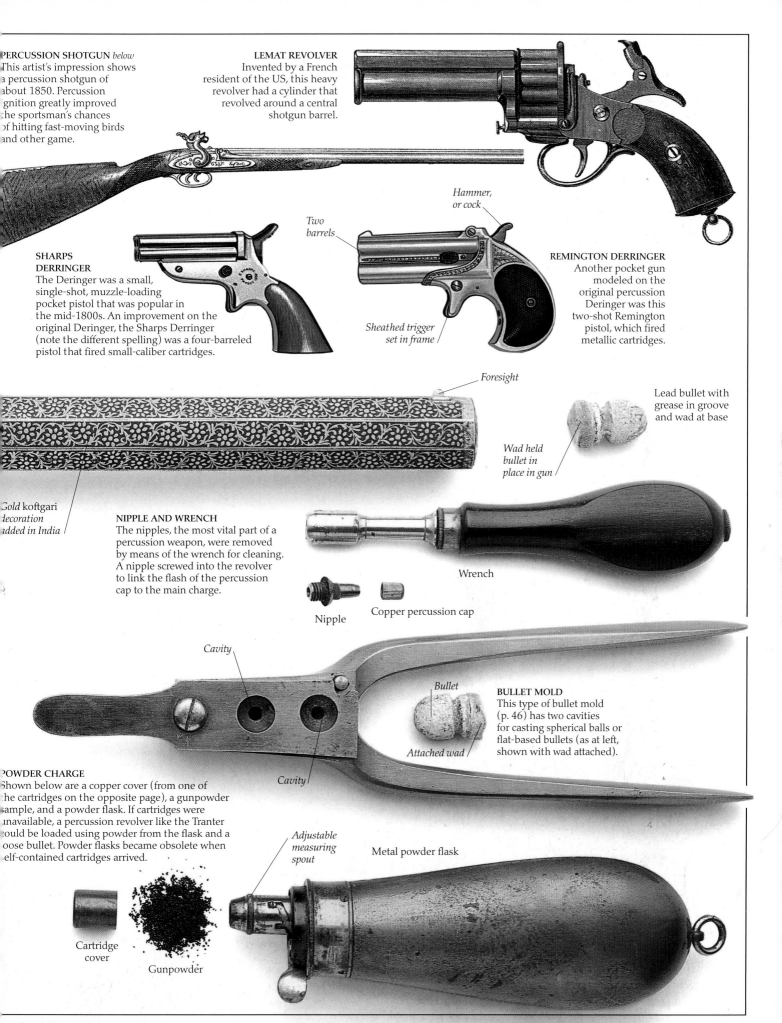

PERCUSSION SHOTGUN *below*
This artist's impression shows a percussion shotgun of about 1850. Percussion ignition greatly improved the sportsman's chances of hitting fast-moving birds and other game.

LEMAT REVOLVER
Invented by a French resident of the US, this heavy revolver had a cylinder that revolved around a central shotgun barrel.

Hammer, or cock

Two barrels

SHARPS DERRINGER
The Deringer was a small, single-shot, muzzle-loading pocket pistol that was popular in the mid-1800s. An improvement on the original Deringer, the Sharps Derringer (note the different spelling) was a four-barreled pistol that fired small-caliber cartridges.

Sheathed trigger set in frame

REMINGTON DERRINGER
Another pocket gun modeled on the original percussion Deringer was this two-shot Remington pistol, which fired metallic cartridges.

Foresight

Lead bullet with grease in groove and wad at base

Wad held bullet in place in gun

Gold koftgari decoration added in India

NIPPLE AND WRENCH
The nipples, the most vital part of a percussion weapon, were removed by means of the wrench for cleaning. A nipple screwed into the revolver to link the flash of the percussion cap to the main charge.

Wrench

Nipple

Copper percussion cap

Cavity

Bullet

BULLET MOLD
This type of bullet mold (p. 46) has two cavities for casting spherical balls or flat-based bullets (as at left, shown with wad attached).

Attached wad

Cavity

POWDER CHARGE
Shown below are a copper cover (from one of the cartridges on the opposite page), a gunpowder sample, and a powder flask. If cartridges were unavailable, a percussion revolver like the Tranter could be loaded using powder from the flask and a loose bullet. Powder flasks became obsolete when self-contained cartridges arrived.

Adjustable measuring spout

Metal powder flask

Cartridge cover

Gunpowder

Guns that won the West

THE WESTWARD EXPANSION of the United States in the 19th century coincided with a period of rapid development in firearms, and the new arms were exploited by settlers, cowboys, Native Americans, the US army, and outlaws alike. The most popular weapons were revolvers, such as those made by Samuel Colt, and repeating rifles, such as the Winchester, which were light enough for use as a carbine on horseback and more accurate than a revolver at longer ranges on the open plains.

Buffalo Bill, holding a Winchester 73,
with the Sioux chief
Sitting Bull

Lever

*Iron
butt-plate*

*Lever incorporated
with trigger guard
pushed forward and
back between shots*

Spare cartridge

Walnut stock

Belt loop

**GUNBELT
AND HOLSTER**
This much-used
19th-century gunbelt
and holster is similar to the
one worn by the US cavalry
officer in campaign dress,
drawn by Frederic Remington
(inset). Note the spare
cartridges in the belt loops.

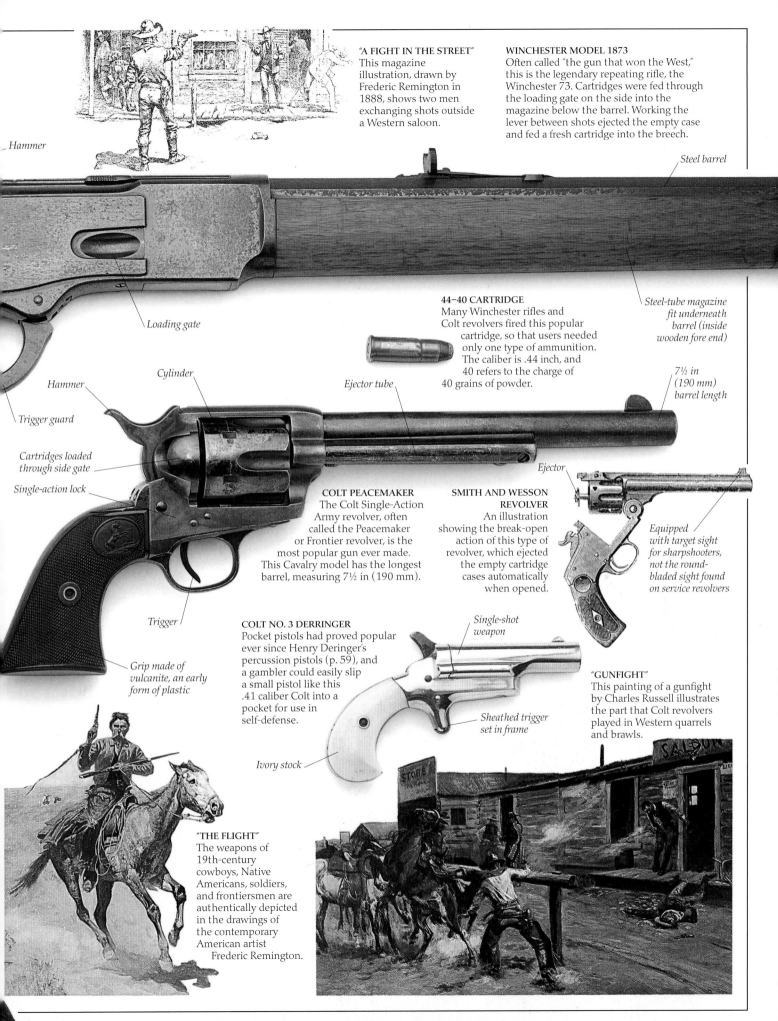

Hammer

"A FIGHT IN THE STREET"
This magazine illustration, drawn by Frederic Remington in 1888, shows two men exchanging shots outside a Western saloon.

WINCHESTER MODEL 1873
Often called "the gun that won the West," this is the legendary repeating rifle, the Winchester 73. Cartridges were fed through the loading gate on the side into the magazine below the barrel. Working the lever between shots ejected the empty case and fed a fresh cartridge into the breech.

Steel barrel

Loading gate

Steel-tube magazine fit underneath barrel (inside wooden fore end)

44–40 CARTRIDGE
Many Winchester rifles and Colt revolvers fired this popular cartridge, so that users needed only one type of ammunition. The caliber is .44 inch, and 40 refers to the charge of 40 grains of powder.

7½ in (190 mm) barrel length

Hammer

Cylinder

Ejector tube

Trigger guard

Cartridges loaded through side gate

Single-action lock

Ejector

COLT PEACEMAKER
The Colt Single-Action Army revolver, often called the Peacemaker or Frontier revolver, is the most popular gun ever made. This Cavalry model has the longest barrel, measuring 7½ in (190 mm).

SMITH AND WESSON REVOLVER
An illustration showing the break-open action of this type of revolver, which ejected the empty cartridge cases automatically when opened.

Equipped with target sight for sharpshooters, not the round-bladed sight found on service revolvers

Trigger

COLT NO. 3 DERRINGER
Pocket pistols had proved popular ever since Henry Deringer's percussion pistols (p. 59), and a gambler could easily slip a small pistol like this .41 caliber Colt into a pocket for use in self-defense.

Single-shot weapon

Grip made of vulcanite, an early form of plastic

Sheathed trigger set in frame

"GUNFIGHT"
This painting of a gunfight by Charles Russell illustrates the part that Colt revolvers played in Western quarrels and brawls.

Ivory stock

"THE FLIGHT"
The weapons of 19th-century cowboys, Native Americans, soldiers, and frontiersmen are authentically depicted in the drawings of the contemporary American artist Frederic Remington.

North American Indians

WRONGLY CALLED *INDIOS* by Christopher Columbus, the native inhabitants of North America once totaled between one and two million people. However, between 1492 and 1900, the Native-American tribes were decimated as European settlers enforced their own way of life on the woodlands and prairies. After initial peaceful contacts with white traders, the tribes that fought hardest to prevent the white man's takeover of their lands in the 1800s were those that lived on the Great Plains and in the southwest. The Plains Indians lived in the central grasslands, where the more nomadic tribes among them hunted the great herds of buffalo that crossed the prairies. Other Native-American tribes, such as the fierce Apaches from the southwest, lived more sedentary lives. Before they obtained European rifles, the tribes in both these areas used the same weapons—bows and arrows (p. 9), knives (pp. 22–23), clubs, and the weapon most strongly associated with the North American Indian—the tomahawk.

A typical mask worn by Indians during religious ceremonies

Finely honed stone blade

STONE-BLADED KNIFE
All Indians owned knives. This one was made in 1900 by a Hupa Indian from California. By 1900, many Indians had steel-bladed knives.

HIAWATHA *left*
An Ojibwa Indian, Hiawatha was the hero of a long narrative poem written in 1855 by Henry Wadsworth Longfellow. In it, Hiawatha becomes leader of his people and teaches peace with the white man.

Feather decoration

Cloth strips bound with buckskin

Quiver made of buckskin

Bow made of ash wood

WAR BOW, c. 1850
Until they began to acquire firearms in the 1850s and 1860s, Plains Indians' bows were their most important weapons, used for both hunting and warfare. Made of ash wood, this bow belonged to a warrior of the Omaha tribe.

Nock, or groove, for attachment of bowstring

Quiver

Bow case

QUIVER AND BOW CASE
For easier carrying on horseback, a Plains Indian had a combined quiver and bow case. Bow accessories were usually made of buckskin or deerskin.

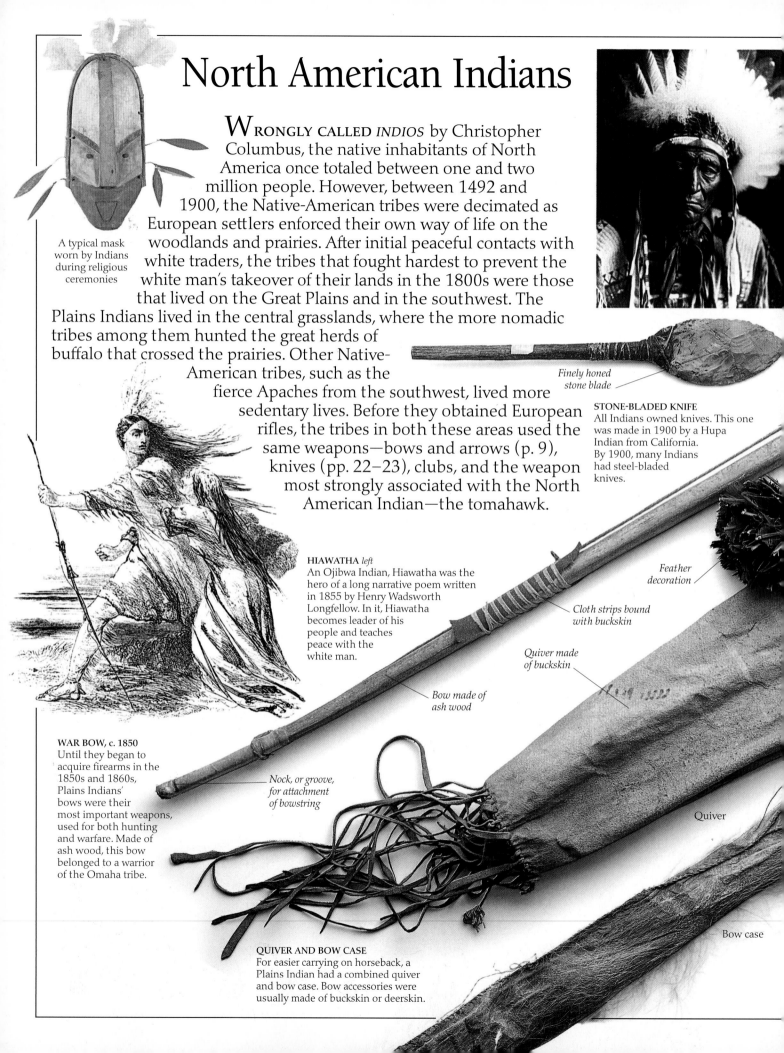

BUFFALO HUNTING
George Catlin spent six years among the Plains Indians, recording their way of life in the early 1800s. In this painting, Indians are involved in their primary hunting task of killing buffalo.

PIPE TOMAHAWK, c. 1890
This pipe tomahawk was supposedly made by the great Apache chief Geronimo, during his exile in Florida.

Tomahawk blade

EAGLE FEATHER HEADDRESS *left*
The eagle feather headdress worn in this photograph of 1907 by Iron Plume, a Plains Indian chieftain, was used for ceremonial occasions. Headdresses were sometimes worn in battle.

Bowstring made of two buffalo sinews twisted together

ARROWS
Plains Indians made arrowheads from buffalo bones. Native Americans in other regions made stone arrowheads.

Feathered flights

Iron tobacco bowl

Wooden shafts were often painted with symbolic designs

Buckskin grip

An Indian with a war club fights another wielding a tomahawk

Engraving of an Indian threatening a European

Iron tobacco bowl

Hollow handle

APACHE PIPE TOMAHAWK, c. 1800 *left*
Before the Native Americans obtained iron from European traders, they made tomahawk heads out of stone. The type of tomahawk that combined an ax blade with a tobacco bowl was usually made by Europeans for trading with the Indians.

Did you know?

AMAZING FACTS

Ordinary Viking warriors typically fought with a long spear. Professional fighters and chieftains used huge, broad-bladed axes. T-shaped axes were usually used for working wood, but the one shown here is so ornate it must have been a weapon and a symbol of prestige or power.

Geometric patterns of inlaid silver
Viking axhead

The Mongol warriors of central Asia were skilled horsemen who could ride up to 75 miles (120 km) a day and hit a target with a bow and arrow at full gallop.

Mongol archers had whistling arrows for signaling, armor-piercing arrows, and even arrows tipped with a kind of explosive grenade. This made them the first warriors to use gunpowder as a weapon.

At one of the largest medieval tournaments ever staged, at Lagny-sur-Marne in France in 1180, more than 3,000 armed and mounted knights fought each other for sport and honor "with no holds barred."

Some jousts were carried out on water. Two teams of rowers propelled their boats toward one another, while a knight standing at the prow (front) of each boat tried to knock his opponent off balance with a lance.

Crossbows and longbows at the Battle of Crecy (1346)

The English longbow, with its range, accuracy, and deadly power, was one of the most decisive weapons of the Middle Ages. It was responsible for the defeat of the French army at Agincourt, France, in 1415, even though the French troops outnumbered the English by five to one.

In 1982, the excavation of the *Mary Rose* shipwreck near Portsmouth, England, revealed 138 preserved longbows. Historians discovered that a longbow's draw power was twice what they had previously thought.

It took years of training and strength to use a longbow effectively, so longbow practice was compulsory by law in England for men of fighting age. This ensured that they maintained their skills in times of peace.

The French would cut three fingers off a captured longbowman's right hand, so that he could not draw his bow again.

Because crossbows were slow to load, crossbowmen sometimes worked in pairs, with one reloading behind a shield (called a pavise) while the other fired.

One of the first soldiers to die in battle from wounds inflicted by a cannon ball was an English soldier at Agincourt, France, in 1415. However, the invention of firearms did not change war all at once. A mixture of swords and pikes alongside muskets and cannon was used in battle throughout the 16th and 17th centuries.

A common weapon among European peasants for several hundred years was a kind of primitive mace called a Morning Star, or Holy Water Sprinkler. This fearsome weapon had an enlarged head made of iron or wood studded with spikes and attached to a long shaft.

Armor was often blued by controlled heating or left black because it was thought to make it less susceptible to rust.

The groove in a sword blade is sometimes wrongly known as a "blood gutter." The groove, or fuller, lightens the blade.

In the 1500s, some rapiers had become extremely long. Queen Elizabeth I of England ordered that rapiers should be broken if they exceeded 3 ft (1 m).

Some early matchlock muskets were so heavy that they had to be fired from a rest. They were, effectively, like small cannons. At the time, cannons were often given the names of animals or birds. "Musket" was the name used by falconers for the male sparrow hawk—the smallest hawk.

Some sword-fighters carried a special weapon in their left hand. This had a serrated edge designed to catch the opponent's rapier blade, which could then be broken with a twist of the wrist.

Mongol archers

After the invention of the wheel-lock, it was possible to make small, easily concealed pistols. Pistols were fitted into the hilts of swords, onto clubs, spears, and crossbows, and even in the handles of knives and forks. Pistols were also combined with other weapons, such as daggers and brass knuckles.

Breastplate left black from the forging process

QUESTIONS AND ANSWERS

Knight in plate battle armor

Q Could a knight in plate armor get up if he fell down on the battlefield?

A A full suit of plate armor weighed around 44–55 lb (20–25 kg). However, its weight was spread over the body, so a fit man could run, lie down, get up, and mount a horse unaided. Stories of cranes being used to winch a knight into his saddle are therefore untrue. The key to a knight's mobility was the way the plates fit together. They were linked by internal straps and pivoting and sliding rivets, so they could move with each other and with the wearer.

Q Did children wear armor in the Middle Ages?

A In Europe, although a boy of noble birth usually started his training to become a knight from the age of seven, he would not have had the money for good-quality armor until he had served his apprenticeship as a squire and had become a knight. This usually happened around the age of 21. However, some rich families did give their young sons gifts of armor. In Japan, ceremonial swords were often given to children when they first put on grown-up or ceremonial clothes.

Q Did animals wear armor, and if so, which ones?

A In battles during the Middle Ages, knights sometimes covered their horses' heads and flanks with mail to protect them as they fought. Plate horse armor was expensive, so usually, if a knight could only afford part of it, he chose the shaffron—the piece for the head. Similarly, hunting dogs were sometimes protected against injury from the tusks of wild boars or stag antlers by quilted, padded vests or, occasionally, by plate and mail. They also wore spiked collars to prevent wolves or other animals from biting their throats. Animal armor was also used in countries outside Europe. For example, in India elephants used in battle were often equipped with protective head and body armor, while the horse armor of the Fulani people of West Africa was made of cotton stuffed with kapok.

Q Do people wear armor today?

A Yes, but although some soldiers wear shiny metal breastplates and carry swords or spears on parade, on the battlefield they wear a type of flak jacket or bulletproof vest and carry guns. Riot police also wear a kind of flak jacket and a protective steel or plastic helmet with a shatterproof visor. Flak jackets are equipped with metal, plastic, or ceramic materials designed to withstand the impact of most types of handgun and some rifle bullets, so the wearer is bruised rather than seriously injured or killed.

Armored elephant

French policeman in riot gear

Q What was the first firearm used in Europe?

A No one knows for sure. However, a manuscript written in England in 1326, called the *Milemete Manuscript*, has a picture of a knight igniting a powder charge in a small cannon shaped like a vase.

Q How were lead bullets made?

A In the 18th century, the bullets, or lead balls, used in flintlock dueling pistols were made at home. Molten lead was poured into a mold; when the lead had cooled, the mold was opened like a pair of scissors and the bullet was removed. Any excess lead was trimmed off using shears.

Record breakers

FIRST BOW AND ARROW
We know from cave paintings that bows and arrows were made and used in the Sahara region of northern Africa from around 30,000 BCE.

LONGEST BOW
The powerful English longbow used from the 13th to 16th centuries was often as tall as its user. With it, an archer's arrows could prove lethal at up to 660 ft (200 m). Some Japanese war bows made of a combination of bamboo and other types of wood were even longer.

FIRST SWORD
The earliest swords were made in about 1500 BCE, at the time when bronze-working was first developed.

LONGEST SWORD
Two-hand swords (large versions of the ordinary sword, swung with both hands) became popular in the 13th century. Some specimens in museums are nearly 6 ft (2 m) long.

INVENTION OF GUNPOWDER
The first recipe for gunpowder was published in 1044 by the Chinese chemist Wu Ching Tsao Yao. The gunpowder was used in fireworks.

LARGEST GUN
The first muskets were the largest guns carried and fired by a single man—some early examples were said to be around 4 ft (1.2 m) long with a bore of 1 in (2.5 cm).

Bronze sword

Who's who?

WE KNOW LITTLE ABOUT THE SKILLED CRAFTSMEN who made early arms and armor, and some famous swordmakers, such as Masamune, rarely signed their work. Later, however, the makers engraved or stamped their names on weapons as a sign of workmanship and quality.

ARMORERS AND SWORDMAKERS

Tsuba

MIOCHIN SCHOOL (c. 1100–c. 1750)
School of Japanese armorers founded in the 12th century by Munesake, famous for its armor and blade guards. Later generations certified work by the school's predecessors that had previously been unsigned.

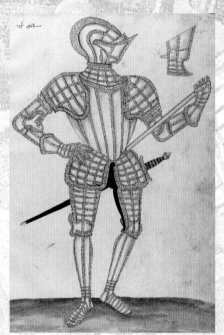

Armor design by Jacobe Halder

MASAMUNE (c. 1265–c. 1358)
Famous Japanese swordmaker of Kamakura, who rarely signed or decorated his sword blades, believing (as did many Japanese swordsmiths) that a fine-quality blade spoke for itself and did not need the maker's mark to prove its worth.

NEGRONI FAMILY (FROM c. 1390)
Family of armorers working in Milan, Italy, that later assumed the family name of Negroli (c. 1521–1580). The Negroli became famous for highly decorated armor, especially embossed armor.

HELMSCHMIDT FAMILY (1445–1532)
Lorenz (1445–1516) and his son Koloman (1471–1532) were armorers based in Augsburg, Germany. They produced armor for the Hapsburg Emperors Maximilian I and Charles V.

TREYTZ FAMILY (c. 1450–1517)
Family of armorers working in Innsbruck, Austria.

SEUSENHOFFER BROTHERS (c. 1459–1519)
Court armorers to Emperor Maximilian I. Conrad Seusenhoffer developed the style of fluted armor known as Maximilian armor.

HANS GRUNEWALT (LATE 1400S)
Nuremberg armorer who worked for Emperor Maximilian I.

HOPFER BROTHERS (c. 1495–1536)
Augsburg engravers who decorated much of the armor made by the Helmschmidts.

NOBUIYE (1496–1564)
Japanese maker of *tsuba* and armor.

JACOB TOPF (1530–1597)
Innsbruck armorer who worked for a time at Greenwich, England.

JACOBE HALDER (c. 1535–1607)
Master armorer at the Greenwich Armory in England.

ANDREA FERRARA (1550–1583)
Italian swordsmith whose blades became popular in Scotland—the famed Highland broadswords are often named after him. Another Italian swordmaker, Giandonato, may have been his brother.

ASSAD ULLAH (c. 1588–1628)
Persian swordsmith whose blades were made of fine steel.

GUNMAKERS

HENRY DERINGER (1786–1868)
American arms maker famous for his distinctive small percussion pistol.

NIKOLAUS VON DREYSE (1787–1867)
German gunsmith who designed a rifle in which bullets were loaded near the trigger. This enabled troops to shoot while lying down, giving them protection from enemy fire.

Samuel Colt

SAMUEL COLT (1814–1862)
American inventor who took out his first patent for a revolver in 1836. He invented several famous models, such as the Colt 45 and the Colt Peacemaker, which is still in use today.

OLIVER WINCHESTER (1810–1880)
Former shirt manufacturer with an interest in firearms who in 1866 founded the Winchester Repeating Arms Company of Connecticut.

PHILO REMINGTON (1816–1889)
American inventor and the son of the inventor Eliphalet Remington, who ran a small-arms factory. Philo managed the factory's mechanical department, becoming president in 1860. He perfected the Remington breech-loading rifle.

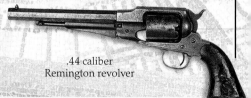

.44 caliber
Remington revolver

RULERS, SOLDIERS, AND HEROES

JULIUS CAESAR (C. 100–44 BCE)
Roman general and statesman whose military campaigns extended Roman power in western Europe. Caesar invaded Britain in 55 and 54 BCE and also defeated the Gauls.

Alexander the Great

ALEXANDER THE GREAT (356–323 BCE)
Son of Philip II of Macedon and tutored by Aristotle, Alexander ascended the throne as King of Macedonia when he was less than 20 years old. During his reign, he conquered Persia, took control of Egypt, and founded the city of Alexandria.

KING ARTHUR (C. 6TH CENTURY)
Legendary king of the Britains represented as a unifier of the British tribes and a champion of Christianity. Arthur is said to have wielded the mythical sword *Excalibur*.

Charlemagne

CHARLEMAGNE (742–814)
King of the Franks who defeated the Saxons, fought the Arabs in Spain, and took control of most of western Europe. He was crowned Roman Emperor in 800 by the pope.

ALFRED THE GREAT (849–899)
King of Wessex, England, who won back land from the Danish invaders. Alfred organized his forces into a standing army and established a network of burhs, or fortified centers, which enabled his successors to secure the unity of England.

WILLIAM I, "THE CONQUEROR" (C. 1028–1087)
Duke of Normandy and the first Norman king of England. In 1066, he defeated and killed the English king Harold II at the Battle of Hastings and replaced Anglo-Saxon leaders with a new ruling class of Normans.

ROBIN HOOD (C. 1220–C. 1350)
Legendary English outlaw and hero, said to be unrivaled with a bow and quarter-staff, who lived in Sherwood Forest with his band of "Merry Men." Unlike later versions, in the original story there is no mention of robbing from the rich to give to the poor, but he does give to a knight in debt.

WILLIAM TELL (C. 1300S)
Legendary Swiss patriot and famous marksman. His killing of the local Austrian steward who had forced him to shoot an apple from his son's head is said to have initiated the movement that secured Switzerland's independence from Austria.

EDWARD, "THE BLACK PRINCE" (1330–1376)
Son of Edward III and a great soldier who fought at the Battle of Crecy (1346) as a teenager. His nickname probably came from the black surcoat he wore for jousting.

HENRY V (1387–1422)
King of England who invaded France in 1415 and won the Battle of Agincourt against great odds, mainly owing to the skill of his longbowmen.

MAXIMILIAN I (1459–1519)
Hapsburg ruler who became Holy Roman Emperor in 1493. His reign saw conflict with France, Switzerland, and Germany. A style of armor with ridges to imitate the pleated clothes worn at the time is named after him, although he does not appear to have connected with it.

HENRY III (1551–1589)
King of France from 1574–1589, whose time as monarch was marked by civil war between the Huguenots and Catholics. He was the last of the French Valois kings.

NAPOLEON BONAPARTE (1769–1821)
French artillery officer who became Emperor of France in 1804. Although defeated by the British navy at Trafalgar (1805), he came to dominate Europe after a series of victories on land. Forced to abdicate when France was invaded, Napoleon regained power but was finally defeated at Waterloo (1815).

DUKE OF WELLINGTON (1769–1852)
British general who was made a duke after his victories against France during the Peninsular War. Along with Prussian forces led by Blücher, his troops defeated the French at the Battle of Waterloo in 1815.

Napoleon Bonaparte

GEBHARD LEBERECHT VON BLÜCHER (1742–1819)
Prussian field marshal who defeated Napoleon Bonaparte at the Battle of Leipzig (1813), then again, with Wellington, at Waterloo (1815). He was known as "Marshal Forward," because his victories were mainly due to the tremendous energy and rapid movement of his troops.

JAMES BOWIE (1796–1836)
American pioneer born in Kentucky and the inventor of the dagger, or sheath knife, named after him. He settled in Texas and became a colonel in the Texan army. Bowie was killed at the Battle of the Alamo in 1836.

WILLIAM FREDERICK CODY, "BUFFALO BILL" (1846–1917)
American army scout and rider for the Pony Express, a mounted mail-delivery service. Cody earned the nickname "Buffalo Bill" after killing 5,000 buffalo as part of a contract to supply railroad workers with meat.

Maximilian armor

Find out more

BECAUSE MOST ARMOR AND WEAPONRY is made of metal, much has survived through the years, and it is still possible to see suits of armor, swords, maces, and other weapons in various museums around the world. There are also many reenactment groups that put on displays to show what warfare was like hundreds of years ago, with members wearing realistic armor and carrying replica arms. You can often see armor and weaponry from earlier periods in history at state ceremonies or official residences, such as that worn by the Swiss Guards at the Vatican City in Rome, Italy (pictured below left).

SEE A FILM
Some movies, such as *Gladiator* (above) or *Braveheart*, show realistic-looking weaponry and armor from different periods in history. The armorers who make the props for these movies often have websites that tell you about their work.

Walnut stock inlaid with engraved staghorn

MUSEUM COLLECTIONS
Most national museums contain impressive displays of arms and armor. For example, the Metropolitan Museum of Art in New York has around 15,000 objects in its collection of arms and armor, including examples from Japan, the Middle East, India, and China. The Musée de l'Armée in Paris, France, contains the French national armor collection and includes many pieces from the 16th century and the Napoleonic era. Some private collections are also open to the public, such as the Wallace Collection in London, England. It is also possible to see arms on display at historic sites such as Colonial Williamsburg in Virginia.

Swiss Guards in Rome, Italy

ARMORIES
Some of the world's great armories—in Vienna, Madrid, Paris, Dresden, and London—have extensive collections where you can see a range of body armor and weapons. The display pictured above shows arms and armor from the 15th to 17th centuries, which is housed in the War Gallery at the Royal Armories Museum in Leeds, England.

DEMONSTRATIONS

The Royal Armouries at the Tower of London, England, sometimes gives members of the public the opportunity to handle both original and replica objects. Many armories also put on demonstrations. For example, the Royal Armouries Museum in Leeds, England, has a Craft Court where it is possible to see armorers, a leather worker, and gunmakers at work using traditional techniques. These craftworkers make many of the replicas used in the museum's hands-on demonstrations. The museum also has a Tiltyard, where performers put on exhibitions of military and sporting skills, such as jousts.

Clothing made by leather workers at Leeds Armoury is worn by staff members, such as the 17th-century-style buffcoat (left)

FIREARMS

Many national museums have collections of firearms. This breech-loading, wheel-lock pistol, on display at the Victoria and Albert Museum in London, England, was made by Hans Stockman in Dresden, Germany, in around 1600.

USEFUL WEBSITES

- View highlights of the museum's vast collection:
  www.metmuseum.org/works_of_art/arms_and_armor
- Visit the National Park Service website for information on armories, battle sites, and arms collections in your area:
  www.nps.org
- For a virtual tour of the British Museum's collection:
  www.britishmuseum.org/explore/highlights.aspx
- Step back in time with epic battles, jousting tournaments, royal feasts, and knights at nine North American locations:
  www.medievaltimes.com

REENACTMENT SOCIETIES

Many different groups in the United Kingdom, other European countries, and the United States, such as the Napoleonic Society, pictured below, reenact scenes or battles from various periods in history. Some societies stage medieval combat or battles from different wars. Find out if any are staging an event near you.

Places to visit

SPRINGFIELD ARMORY, SPRINGFIELD, MASSACHUSSETS

This historic site offers the story of the nation's first armory. The museum highlights many of the best examples of US military shoulder arms plus pistols, machine guns, edged weapons, and production machinery. View the cases and look at a rare 14th century hand gun, a modern Vulcan 20 mm Gatling Gun, or see the revolutionary 1822 Blanchard stockmaking lathe.

HIGGINS ARMORY MUSEUM, WORCESTER, MASSACHUSSETS

This museum has five floors displaying more than 8,000 pieces of armor and weaponry. Different galleries are devoted to the tournament, hunting, ancient arms and armor, the armorer's craft, and arms and armor from around the world. There is also a combat wing.

THE METROPOLITAN MUSEUM OF ART, NEW YORK, NEW YORK

The collection of armor, edged weapons, and firearms ranks with those of other great armories of the world. Approximately 15,000 objects range in date from 400 BC to the 19th century. Western Europe and Japan are the regions most strongly represented—the collection of more than 5,000 pieces of Japanese armor and weapons is the finest outside Japan—although the geographical range of the collection is extraordinary. The focus is on outstanding craftsmanship and decoration.

COLONIAL WILLIAMSBURG, WILLIAMSBURG, VIRGINIA

The Colonial Arms display highlights weapons from the Revolutionary War period, while the Lock, Stock, and Barrel collection features a complete lineage of arms from the 18th century to the Napoleonic wars. At the gunsmith's shop, visitors can watch a master gunsmith demonstrate the skills required to build a gun.

BUFFALO BILL HISTORICAL CENTER, CODY, WYOMING

More than 6,000 objects chronicle the technological development of firearms, from the earliest incarnations to the most modern forms. The Winchester Collection forms the heart of the most comprehensive assemblage of American firearms in the world.

Helmet found at Sutton Hoo, on display at the British Museum in London, England

Glossary

Artilleryman

ARMORER Metalworker specializing in making armor. In Europe, the craft of the armorer was regulated by a guild.

ARTILLERY Originally, "artillery" meant any machine used to throw stones and other missiles, later it was used for cannon.

BASINET Helmet, popular during the 14th century. Some basinets had a plate visor to protect the face (*see also* VISOR).

BAYONET Blade designed to fit into or over a gun muzzle.

BLUNDERBUSS Short gun or pistol with a large bore and a wide muzzle that fired a number of small shots.

BOLT Short, heavy arrow used with the crossbow. A bolt with a four-sided head was sometimes known as a quarrel (*see also* CROSSBOW).

BREECH LOADER Firearm loaded from the breech, or back part, of the gun rather than from the muzzle at the front.

BROADSWORD Military sword with a wide, straight blade.

BURGONET Helmet originating in Burgundy, worn by cavalrymen and infantry officers in the 16th century.

Burgonet

CARBINE Lightweight rifle with a short barrel, originally developed for use by cavalry or as a saddle firearm for horse riders. It also later became an infantry weapon.

CAVALRY Mounted soldiers, often divided into two main groups—light cavalry (whose main tasks were scouting and pursuit of a beaten enemy), and heavy cavalry (used for shock impact, that is, charging in solid lines).

CLAYMORE Double-edged, two-hand broadsword with a long, heavy blade. Claymores were used by Scottish Highlanders in the 15th and 16th centuries. The name comes from the Gaelic *claidheamohmor*, meaning "great sword."

CROSSBOW Popular weapon in medieval Europe, in which a cord was drawn back to shoot arrows called bolts or quarrels. Most crossbows were so powerful that mechanical means were needed to span, or draw, them.

CUIRASS Type of body armor comprising a breastplate and backplate worn together and usually fastened by straps or buckles. Originally made of leather, cuirasses were later made of bronze, then steel.

DAGGER Small version of a sword with a short blade and a sharp point.

DUELING PISTOL High-quality, muzzle-loading pistol, usually supplied in a box as a pair, along with accessories for making bullets, cleaning, and loading.

FENCING Refers to the art and skill of fighting with a rapier, developed in France and Italy in the early 17th century.

FLAIL Weapon consisting of a bar attached to a haft by a swivel, or one or more balls attached by chain. All types of flail could be studded with spikes (*see also* MACE).

FLINTLOCK Type of gun, introduced in about 1630, in which a flint is struck against a steel hammer, sending sparks into the priming powder and igniting the main charge. The lock, or ignition system, had to be set to the "full-cock" position before the gun could be fired, making it safer to use.

FULLER Groove down the length of a sword to lighten the blade.

GAUNTLET Hand armor.

GLADIUS Short, double-edged thrusting sword used by Roman infantry.

GORGET In European plate armor, a collar plate that protects the neck.

GREAVE European armor for the lower leg, at first just for the shin, but later also including a part to protect the calf.

Dagger

GRENADIERS Originally troops trained to use hand grenades, grenadiers wore low caps which made it easier for them to sling a musket over their shoulder, leaving both hands free to light and throw a grenade. By the 19th century, the word grenadier was used to refer to ordinary infantry troops.

GUILD Medieval association that controlled and regulated a particular craft, such as armor-making (*see also* PROOF).

HALBERD Type of staff weapon consisting of a long wooden handle mounted with an ax blade, backed by a hook, and topped by a spike.

HAND GRENADE Hollow iron ball filled with explosive and threaded with a short fuse. The first hand grenades came into use in the 17th century (*see also* GRENADIERS).

HARNESS Full suit of armor.

Mempo

HAUBERK Long tunic made of mail.

HELM Helmet that completely enclosed the head and face, used from the early 1200s.

HILT End of a sword, comprising a grip, a pommel for balance, and often a hand guard.

INFANTRY Foot soldiers.

JOUST Contest in which two charging knights tried to dismount each other with lances. Later the goal was to score points by breaking your lance against your opponent (*see also* TOURNAMENT).

KABUTO Japanese helmet.

KATANA Long fighting sword used by Japanese samurai.

KRIS Malaysian knife with a range of blade shapes, hilts, and scabbards.

LONGBOW Tall, powerful bow used in Europe in the Middle Ages and usually made from one piece of shaped and honed yew wood. Yew from the heartwood (which resists compression) and the sapwood (which resists tension), formed a strong, natural spring.

MACE Weapon with a haft and a metal head. Some heads were spiked. Others were ridged to penetrate armor (*see also* FLAIL).

MATCHLOCK Gun with an early, simple firing mechanism in which an S-shaped lever was pressed down to force a match into a flashpan that ignited the powder. This was later replaced by the flintlock.

MAXIMILIAN ARMOR Name given to a style of 16th-century plate armor with narrow fluting that was popular during the reign of Holy Roman Emperor, Maximilian I.

MEMPO Japanese face armor, which was sometimes decorated to resemble the face of an old man, a demon, or a ghost.

MORION HELMET Type of lightweight, open helmet—often made of a single piece of steel—with a broad brim and peak, and also cheek pieces. Popular in the mid-16th century, this was worn mainly by infantry.

MUSKET Originally, a matchlock gun that was fired from a rest because of its great weight. Later, the word "musket" came to mean any gun used by infantry.

MUSKETEER Infantry soldier armed with a musket.

PAULDRON Piece of European plate armor covering the shoulder.

PAVISE Large wooden shield used to protect archers and crossbowmen when loading and firing their weapons.

PERCUSSION LOCK Type of firearm ignition introduced in the early 1800s. A hammer hits a detonating mixture that explodes and ignites the main charge that fires the bullet.

Guild marks from Umbria, Italy

PIKEMAN Infantry soldier usually armed with a pike, or long spear, a sword, and a buckler (shield). In the 17th century, pikemen were protected from musket fire by a morion helmet and a cuirass.

POMMEL Shaped weight on the hilt of a sword to balance the weight of the blade. The name comes from the French word "pomme," meaning apple.

PROOF To test armor by firing a crossbow bolt at it from short range and later a musket. Proofed pieces were sometimes stamped with the maker's or guild's mark.

RAPIER Sword with a sharp point, usually with a complex hilt covering the hand and bars protecting the knuckles.

SABATON Foot armor covering the upper side of the foot and secured by straps and/or laces.

SABER Cavalry sword with a single-edged, slightly curving blade.

SHAFFRON Armor for a horse's head.

SHAMSHIR Lightweight hunting sword originating in Persia, later called a scimitar.

SMALLSWORD Light form of the rapier, with a triangular blade designed for thrusting. Used from the late 1600s until the late 1700s, when they were known as "town" or "walking" swords because they were mostly used as fashion accessories.

SPUR Point attached to the heel of a rider used to speed up a horse. Often seen as the badge of knighthood (from the saying "when a knight won his spurs").

STILETTO Small dagger with a slender blade designed for thrusting.

TILT Barrier introduced in the 15th century to separate jousting knights.

TOURNAMENT Mock fight originally meant to train men for war, it later became a display of fighting skills with complex rules. It included the tourney or melée (between two groups that fought on horseback), the joust, and, later, the foot combat.

TSUBA Japanese sword guard.

Shaffron

TULWAR Curved Indian sword.

VAMBRACE European plate armor worn on the arm.

VISOR Protective armor for the face, introduced around 1300, which was hinged and could be swung up. Some visors could be detached from the helmet for cleaning or for repair (*see also* HELMET).

WAKIZASHI Short Japanese sword used as a second fighting sword by a samurai warrior (after the *katana*).

WHEEL-LOCK Gun with a later form of ignition than the matchlock, in which sparks from a spinning wheel were showered into the pan, thereby setting off the charge. The wheel-lock was later replaced by the flintlock (*see also* FLINTLOCK).

WINDLASS Mechanism with pulleys and handles that fit over the butt of a crossbow, enabling the crossbow's cord to be wound back tightly, ready for shooting (*see also* CROSSBOW).

Jousting knights

Index

Acknowledgments

Dorling Kindersley would like to thank:
City of London Police: pp.54–55; also Police Constable Ray Hayter for his assistance; Pitt Rivers Museum, University of Oxford, Oxford: pp.4–5, 22–23, 32–33, 36–37; also John Todd for his assistance; Ermine Street Guard: pp.1, 12–13; also Nicholas Fuentes for his assistance; Museum of London: pp.6–7, 10–11, 12bl, 14–15; also Nick Merriman, Peter Stott, and Gavin Morgan for their assistance; Museum of Mankind, British Museum: pp.8–9, 62–63; National Army Museum: pp.56–57; also Stephen Bull for his help; Warwick Castle, Warwick: pp.16–17, 24–25, 26–27, 28–29, 30–31, 38–39, 40–41, 42–43, 44–45, 48–49, 52–53, 55t; also F.H.P. Barker for his assistance; Robin Wigington, Arbour Antiques, Ltd, Stratford-upon-Avon: pp.2–3, 18–19, 20–21, 34–35, 38b, 50–51, 58–59, 60–61; Anne-Marie Bulat for her work on the initial stages of the book; Martyn Foote for design assistance; Fred Ford and Mike Pilley of Radius Graphics, and Ray Owen and Nick Madren for artwork; Jonathan Buckley for his help on the photographic sessions; Coral Mula for the illustration on p.6.
Proofreading Caitlin Doyle
Wall chart Peter Radcliffe, Steve Setford

Clipart CD Jo Little, Lisa Stock, Jessamy Wood

Picture credits
The publisher would like to thank the following for their kind permission to reproduce their photographs:

(Key: a-above; b-below/bottom; c-center; f-far; l-left; r-right; t-top)

Lesley and Roy Adkins: 64–65; The Art Archive: 70tl; Bibliotheque Nationale Paris 64bl; British Library: 70–71; Museo dell'Opera del Duomo Orvieto/Dagli Orti 71tc; Oriental Art Museum Genoa/Dagli Orti 66tr; Reproduced by Courtesy of the Trustees of the British Museum: 14bc; The Board of Trustees of the Armouries: 65tr, 68br, 69tr; Bridgeman Art Library, London/New York: British Library 64cr, 65tl; The Stapleton Collection 71bl; Victoria & Albert Museum 68–69c; Victoria & Albert Museum, London 66cl; British Museum: cr, 69br, 70tr; Corbis: Ali Meyer 67bl; Araldo de Luca 66–67, 67tl; Michael S. Yamashita 68–69; Philadelphia Museum of Art 70bl; Sygma/Graham Tim 68bl;

Danish National Museum: 64tl; E. T. Archives: 8b; English Heritage: Paul Lewis 69b Gettysburg National Military Park: 66br; Giraudon: 43tl; Goteborg Museum of Art: 39c; India Office Library (British Library): 33t. John Freeman London: 16br; 18c, tr; 19cr; 21tr; 26b; 28cr, bl; 30tc; 31t; 39t; 40c; 42b; 44tl; 52t; 53b; 54t; 62tl, tr, cl H. Josse, Paris: 44b; Kobal Collection: Dreamworks/Universal/ Buitendijk, Jaap 68tl; Mansell Collection: 11m; 42c; Mary Evans Picture Library: 6b; 7bl; 8c; 9b; 12t, br; 13t, b; 14bl; 16bl, t; 17tr, tr; 19t; 20t, c, b; 22t, c; 23c; 24b; 25c, b; 26tl, tr; 27b; 28cc; 29bl, br; 30c, tl, tr; 34tl; 35t; 36c; 38c; b; 39b; 40tl; 44tr; 47tr, b; 48c; 49c, b; 51c; 52tr, c; 54t, b; 55c, b; 56t; 57tl, tr; 58tl, tr, b; 60b; 61c, t, 66bl; Michael Holford: 12bl, 15t, c, b; 32b; 36–37; 63t; Museum of London: 65br; National Army Museum: 53t; Peter Newark's Western Americana and Historical Pictures: 14br; 29c; 37c; 41b; 46t; 47tl; 56b; 60t; 61br; 63b; Rex Features: 65bc; Robert Hunt Library: 21c; Sheridan Photo Library: 7br; Tower of London Royal Armouries: 25t; Visual Arts Library: 43tr, c; 61bl; The Wallace Collection: 64br, 67br, 71cr.

Wall chart:
Alamy Images: Robert Harding Picture Library/Adam Woolfit ftr; **Dorling Kindersley:** Courtesy of the City of London Police clb (handcuffs), clb (rattle), clb (truncheon); Courtesy of the Ermine Street Guard tr; Courtesy of The Museum of London fcla (flint), fcla (handax), fcl (Viking); Courtesy of the National Army Museum, London fcrb (bag); Courtesy of the Pitt Rivers Museum, University of Oxford fbl; Courtesy of The Wallace Collection, London c; Courtesy of Warwick Castle, fclb (backsword), fclb (hunting), cr (pouch), fcrb (flintlock); Courtesy of Robin Wigington, Arbour Antiques, Ltd, Stratford-upon-Avon fcr (firearms), fcl (claymore), fcra (battle-ax), fcra (knife), fcrb (cartridges), fcrb (pepperbox), fcrb (repeating); Museum of Mankind/British Museum fbr, ftl; **Getty Images:** Bibliotheque Nationale, Paris, France/Bridgeman Art Library cla (Turkish archers).

Jacket:
Front: **Ermine Street Guard**, UK, b; **National Army Museum**, London, UK, tl; **Warwick Castle**, UK, cl; **Museum of Mankind**, UK, tc; **Bettmann/Corbis**, tcr; **Pitt Rivers Museum**, Oxford, UK, tr (ALB only).
Back: **Pitt Rivers Museum**, Oxford, UK, tl; **Robin Wigington, Arbour Antiques**, cl; **Warwick Castle**, bl; **Museum of London**, tr.

All other images © Dorling Kindersley.
For further information see:
www.dkimages.com